The Homeric Scholia
and the *Aeneid*

The Homeric Scholia
and the Aeneid

A Study of the Influence of
Ancient Homeric Literary Criticism on Vergil

Robin R. Schlunk

Ann Arbor

The University of Michigan Press

PA6825
S44

This book is published with aid from the Classics
Fund of the University of Cincinnati, a Gift of
Louise Taft Semple, in Memory of Charles Phelps Taft.

To C. R. T.

Preface

Some years ago, Hermann Fränkel attempted to demonstrate that Livius Andronicus made use of the Homeric scholia while translating the *Odyssey* into Latin. Towards the conclusion of his article, "Griechische Bildung in altrömischen Epen," in *Hermes* 67 (1932), pp. 307–8, Fränkel stated that:

> Translation is in itself an act of interpretation, and just as every translation falls short of the original in many respects so, too, it is necessary that each one in its various interpretations must go outside the original.

If this view is acceptable, it would naturally follow that Homeric criticism and exegesis prior to his own time would have had some effect upon Vergil's understanding and appreciation of the *Iliad* and the *Odyssey*, for although in no way can the *Aeneid* be regarded as a mere translation of the Homeric epics, it can in many passages and episodes be regarded as a subjective and new reinterpretation of them.

It has long been axiomatic that Vergil wrote under the influence of Alexandrian poetry and the literary tastes and theories which produced it. These tastes and theories would not only be indirectly apparent from the Hellenistic poetry which Vergil is assumed to have imitated, but they would also be directly expressed in the literary commentaries and criticisms of the Alexandrian as well as Pergamene scholars, especially those which are now preserved in the scholia on the Homeric poems. These Homeric scholia, considered as a corpus, comprise the best single source now extant for our knowledge of Alexandrian literary criticism in practice.

Though a thorough investigation in this area of possible influence on the *Aeneid* has not hitherto been made, there has been some recognition of the need for it. The eminent Vergilian scholar, Richard Heinze (*Virgils Epische Technik*, 3rd ed., Leipzig, 1914), appears to have been the first to intimate that Vergil might have considered and, indeed, been influenced by the Homeric scholia during his composition of the *Aeneid* (see his index, "Homerscholien" and especially p. 164, n. 1). More recently, Georg Knauer in his *Die Aeneis und Homer* (Göttingen, 1964; see pp. 68, n. 1; 168, n. 2; 356, n. 1) explicitly pointed to the lack of such a study and stressed the need especially for an examination of the allegorical scholia and their relationship to Vergil's understanding of the Homeric poems.

The purpose of this investigation, then, is to examine an aspect of Vergil's technique of imitation in the *Aeneid*, and to attempt to demonstrate an indebtedness to Hellenistic literary criticism on various types of passages which he appropriated from the Homeric poems. Although this investigation is in no way comprehensive, it is hoped that the variety and extent of the passages, similes, and in some cases whole episodes, all of which will be compared and analyzed in the light of the Homeric scholia, will afford new insight into some of the many subtle and virtually imperceptible changes which Vergil so often made in his prototypes. It is hoped, too, that this study will help to further an understanding of Vergil's assimilative powers, and above all, of his originality, for it is indeed in his imitation that Vergil's originality can best be appreciated.

There remain three difficulties which warrant brief mention; the first, and certainly most crucial, is the vexed, if not insoluble, problem of assigning origins to the anonymous scholia, especially those of the so-called BT group. It is some consolation to know that many of these scholia are thought to derive from the Stoic, or Pergamene School, but for a study of this type, this theory, unfortunately, must remain purely conjectural. On the other hand, many of the comments of the A scholia are demonstrably Alexandrian, and on occasion both groups cite Aristotle as the ultimate source. In short, somewhat more than one third of the scholia cited in this study clearly stem from the *floruit* of Hellenistic Homeric scholarship, and as such, would have been readily available to Vergil. As for those scholia which bear no indication of their origin, all will be seen to be quite in keeping both in tone and spirit with those which can be dated, and will, I trust, be acceptable as supporting evidence.

Since the scholia are very often extremely terse and at times even cryptic, I have attempted to render almost literal translations into English rather than to paraphrase them and so possibly place them in a tendentious light. Where the remarks are lengthy and easy to follow, I have felt at liberty simply to note the essence of their contents.

It is, of course, impossible to render incontrovertible conclusions on so complex and unfathomable a subject as poetic genius. To use the words of L. A. MacKay as they appeared in his article entitled "Achilles as a Model for Aeneas," *TAPA* 88 (1957), p. 11:

> In the most delicate, and some of the most important problems of literary influence, it is seldom possible to say what happened, or even if we are careful with our language, what must have happened. We can guess at what probably happened, but what seems plausible to one may seem extremely unlikely to another. What look like echoes may be mere coincidences. We must be wary of implying that no poet had an original idea since Orpheus.

Surely Vergil's own responsiveness to the Homeric poems must not be overlooked in any study of his variations on Homeric themes, yet his reputation as a poet and scholar and the very nature of his poetry make it seem more than likely that he would have consulted the well-known and highly respected commentaries of the Hellenistic scholars in the course of his study and use of the *Iliad* and the *Odyssey*. This is certainly not to imply that Vergil would have felt constrained to abide by the *dicta* of the ancient scholars, but it is not unlikely that in certain cases he found their critical and exegetical remarks not only perceptive, but even suggestive and useful in creating an epic worthy to be ranked with those of Homer.

I wish to express my thanks to the University of Chicago Press and to Harper and Row Publishers, for their kindness in allowing me to use Professor Richmond Lattimore's translations of the *Iliad* and the *Odyssey*, respectively. I wish also to thank the readers of the University of Michigan Press for their many suggestions which have been extremely useful, and my wife for her help in organizing several difficult parts of the exposition. Finally, I wish to express my deepest and most sincere gratitude to Professor Carl R. Trahman of the University of Cincinnati for his suggestion of this subject as a dissertation topic, for his kindness and help in its original execution, and for his continued help and encouragement.

Contents

I

Vergil and the Homeric Scholia

Vergil was said in antiquity to have been a meticulous scholar and conscientious craftsman, and it is clear from the allusions in his poetry that he was an extremely learned man. We do not need the testimony of the ancient *vitae* or of Quintilian or of Macrobius to substantiate either of these points.[1] There can likewise be no doubt that Vergil not only imitated Homer throughout the whole of the *Aeneid*, but at the same time sought to rival his predecessor both in the overall purpose of his epic as well as in the finest and most minute of poetic details.[2] On the other hand, it is also well known that Vergil was most familiar with all the recognized masterpieces of Greek and Roman literature and so skillful and often subtle was his adaptation and integration of earlier poetry into his own work that ancient scholars, no less than modern, were occasionally hard put to track down the sources of his inspiration, as in fact Macrobius noted (*Sat.* V. 18, 1):

> fuit enim hic poeta, ut scrupulose et anxie, ita dissimulanter et clanculo doctus, ut multa transtulerit, quae unde translata sint difficile sit cognitu.

It is easy to imagine that one reason for the difficulty in determining the sources for what might appear to be poetic borrowings, yet at the same time are so sufficiently different as to preclude ready recognition, is that Vergil, though eager to exploit literary associations already in the mind of the reader, would nevertheless have done his utmost to improve upon the work of his predecessors in whatever way his own poetic genius might inspire him.

Let us assume that Vergil was well aware that he would be compared with Homer.[3] If this is the case, as it would appear, it is not difficult to suppose that in the course of his study of the Homeric poems, if not in the actual course of his composition of the *Aeneid*, Vergil would have carefully examined the critical literature that had grown up around the *Iliad* and the *Odyssey* in the previous several generations.

It might legitimately be asked whether so accomplished a poet and scholar of literature as Vergil would have had recourse to so vast and rambling a collection of comments as those which comprise the scholia as we know them today, especially in view of the fact that on occasion much of the critical and exegetical work of the Alexandrians in particular has been brushed aside as so much misapplied logic. "Misapplied logic" may frequently exist, especially from our point of view, and so it may often have seemed to Vergil who did not hesitate to appropriate passages athetized by the Alexandrians. And yet many of these same passages appear in the *Aeneid* with significant changes, some of which seem to have been suggested, if not by the particular arguments of the scholiasts, then at least by their critical temper. Finally, it has also been charged that the Alexandrians were virtually obsessed with principles of decorum. It is nonetheless true that one of the primary underlying differences between the Homeric epics and the *Aeneid* is precisely that the Roman poet reveals a far greater preoccupation with just these principles—one need only think of Horace and his *Ars Poetica*.[4] What now may appear to be of little significance as literary commentary might well once have been considered of great importance: to a scholarly temperament such as Vergil's, we may rightly assume that nothing that might possibly have aided him in his composition would have been regarded as unworthy of his consideration.

The Alexandrian scholars were highly esteemed in antiquity and known to Roman *litterati*, perhaps even from the time of Livius Andronicus, and there is certainly more than ample evidence that they and their works were well known to contemporaries of Vergil.[5] The grammatical works of Aristarchus were known and referred to by Varro.[6] Cicero also refers to him several times, and in one instance appears to use his name as a synonym for any astute literary critic (*ad Att.* I. 14, 3):

> quid multa? totum hunc locum, quem ego varie meis orationibus, quarum tu Aristarchus es, soleo pingere, de flamma, de ferro (nosti illas λημύθους), valde graviter pertexuit.[7]

Horace also used his name in similar fashion in the well-known statement of his *Ars Poetica* (445–50):

> vir bonus et prudens versus reprehendet inertis,
> culpabit duros, incomptis allinet atrum
> traverso calamo signum, ambitiosa recidet
> ornamenta, parum claris lucem dare coget,
> arguet ambigue dictum, mutanda notabit,
> fiet Aristarchus. . . .

In themselves such references prove only that Aristarchus was well known by name, yet there is some additional evidence that both Horace and Cicero made use of Alexandrian readings in their references to the Homeric poems.

While discussing Aristarchus's methods of textual criticism, Van der Valk cites an example which occurs in the description of the portent at Aulis. The serpent has devoured the birds (*Il.* II. 317 ff.):

> After he had eaten the sparrow herself with her children the god who had shown the snake forth made him a *monument*, striking him ¡stone, the son of devious-devising Kronos, and we standing about marvelled at the thing that had been done.

Aristarchus, disagreeing with Zenodotus's reading of ἀρίδηλον (*monument*, lit., "conspicuous"), chose rather to read ἀΐζηλον ("unseen") and athetized the following line (319) as a later interpolation to explain ἀρίδηλον.[8] Cicero translated the lines as follows (*De Div.* II. 30, 64):

> hunc, ubi tam teneros volucris matremque peremit
> qui luci ediderat, genitor Saturnius idem
> *abdidit* et duro formavit tegmine saxi.
> nos autem, timidi stantes. . . .

As Van der Valk points out, Cicero retained the line which Aristarchus athetized, yet chose to include his reading of ἀΐζηλον (*idem/abdidit*) over that of Zenodotus. On the other hand, it could be argued that Cicero made his translation from a "hybrid" text which had already incorporated Aristarchus's conjecture. Whether direct or indirect, the influence of Aristarchus on interpretations of Homer in Augustan times remains clear, if only for his readings of individual words.

Tolkiehn, moreover, believed that Horace chose Zenodotus's reading of νόμον ("custom") for νόον ("mind," "thought") in his translation of *Od.* I. 3 in *Epist.* I. 2, 20:[9]

> Many were they whose cities he saw, whose *minds* he learned of . . .
> qui [Ulixes] domitor Troiae multorum providus urbis
> et *mores* hominum inspexit. . . .

Such an interpretation of νόον, however, as the equivalent of *mores* might easily derive from the word itself, as the E scholium implies:

> νόον ἔγνω) . . . πρακτικός, ὡς ὅταν τις ἰδὼν πολλὰς πόλεις καὶ χώρας κἀκείνων γενόμενος ἔμπειρος ἐξ ἐκείνων γνῶσιν συνάξῃ.

> In a practical sense, as when someone, when he has seen many cities and places and has gained experience from them, as a result of this accumulates knowledge.

Granted, then, that Alexandrian scholarship commanded authority and respect throughout antiquity; yet the question arises: what were the media of its diffusion and the opportunities for studying it that might have been available to Roman scholars? It is true that the whole corpus of scholia as they now exist derives from excerpts of commentaries compiled by scholars of the early Roman empire. These scholars in turn had incorporated into their own work the textual and exegetical criticisms of the Alexandrian commentators.[10] Foremost among these scholars was Didymus Chalcenterus, whose work continued that of Aristarchus.

There remains some strong evidence that these scholarly works of the Alexandrians were published in separate form, though they might also have existed in the margins of texts of the Homeric poems which the Romans read. In an address entitled "The Study of Homer in Greco-Roman Egypt" delivered in 1955, J. A. Davison, while discussing in part the kinds and qualities of the Homeric texts represented in the Egyptian papyrus fragments, pointed to one which consists of only the subscription of a text:

> Ἀπολλοδώϱ[ου]/ Ἀθηναίου/ γϱαμματιϰ[οῦ]/ ζητήματ[α]/
> γϱαμματιϰ[ὰ]/ [ε]ἰς τ[ὴν]/ ξ/ τῆς Ἰ[λ]ιάδ[ος]/ Σωσύου.

The Critical Inquiries of Apollodorus of Athens on the Fourteenth Book of the *Iliad*, Sosius's.

The suggestion was then made that this fragment might be evidence that such commentaries and monographs were still being published by the Sosii, well known as booksellers in Horace's time.[11]

Be that as it may, there is ample evidence that commentaries were being written on Homer as early as the fourth century; indeed, there is some indication that allegorical interpretations began as early as the sixth century B.C. Still, it is with Aristotle that the great *floruit* seems to have begun, and although his *Homeric Problems* has been lost, fragments of it are preserved in the scholia, especially in passages extracted from Porphyry. It might also be added that other books of a similar nature were written, among them one of the same title by Zeno the Stoic, whose work, presumably, contained allegorical interpretations of the Homeric poems. His investigations were continued by Cleanthes and Crates of Pergamum who, according to Suetonius, first introduced Greek literary criticism to Rome.[12]

Aside from the legitimate scholarly investigations into such literary problems as Homer's dates, the authorship of the poems, dialect, grammar, contradictions within the poems, and so forth, it appears that such questions or "problems" became popular as topics of "after dinner conversation": one need only think of Athenaeus's *Deipnosophistae* and Macrobius's *Saturnalia*. There is also some indication that such problems were raised simply for the pleasure of exercising one's wits in providing ingenious solutions. It is doubtless that today's *enstatikoi* became tomorrow's *lutikoi*. The form of many of the scholia on the Homeric poems seems based on this type of exercise: the question is first posed and the answer or answers follow.

As they stand in the scholia, many of these questions and answers appear to have been taken over from texts *in usum scholarum*, as it were, yet as has been noted, we know that serious commentaries and monographs were written on just these problems. Whatever these works might have been, we may be certain that they were in a different form from the comments which now survive in the scholia.

Finally, it appears that the Servian commentaries on the *Aeneid* show a dependence on the Homeric scholia not only, as Eduard Fraenkel has demonstrated, ". . . for a great deal of their subject matter but also for their method of argumentation."[13] In several instances it is quite clear that Servius has interpreted passages in the *Aeneid* which were unquestionably drawn from the *Iliad* in the light of the Greek commentaries still extant in the scholia. Most interesting in this respect is the fact that Vergil appears to have altered a few of these passages in the *Aeneid* so as to conform with the scholiasts' suggestions as to how Homer might "better" have presented the lines under discussion.[14] It would seem highly unlikely that such a close correspondence between Vergil's interpretation of Homer as it appears in the *Aeneid*, the comments of the scholiasts, and Servius's interpretation of Vergil is purely coincidental. Certainly, what was known to Latin scholars several generations after the composition of the *Aeneid* was known to Vergil and to all learned readers of the *Aeneid* as well. Herein lies the crux of the matter: Vergil assumed a thorough knowledge of the *Iliad* and the *Odyssey* in his readers, but he also assumed that they possessed a general acquaintance with the traditional Homeric literary criticism. Whatever allusions he might make to Homeric imagery, characterization, and action would be immediately recognized, and as a result the purpose of any variations he might choose to make on Homeric themes would be more readily understood by his readers. Vergil was not writing in a vacuum of literary criticism, and it is clear from the scholia that certain Homeric episodes, for example, had become exemplars of right or wrong action and that certain similes and images had taken on symbolic meanings which were known to most, if not all, learned readers of the *Iliad* and *Odyssey*. Whenever Vergil chose to use, or indeed adapt, such Homeric passages, his purpose would surely become more explicit.

It is upon this interpretative foundation that Vergil partly based the understanding of his epic. It is also with a similar knowledge of Homeric scholarship and exegesis as can be gleaned from the scholia that we, too, can best appreciate his purpose and especially his originality in his adaptations of Homeric themes.

II

The Scholia and the Aeneid: *Propriety*

Like their modern counterparts, scholars in antiquity were
often struck by Vergil's use of Homeric lines, similes, and even
incidents totally removed from their original context. The
Verona scholium to *Aeneid* X. 557 is a case in point:

> Sic in quibusdam dum nimio studio Vergilius ad Homerum
> trahitur, neque temporis neque loci habet curam.

This judgment, while natural enough for scholars overwhelmed
by many hundreds of such borrowings, is erroneous. The fact
is that Vergil was extremely careful in expropriating Homeric
lines in or out of context as the subsequent discussion will
attempt to show.

Of the miscellaneous Homeric passages that follow, some
were condemned by the Alexandrians on the grounds of impropriety (whether social or literary), others merely contain
obscure words which required explication, and some were simply
admired and commented upon for their effect. Vergil has carefully harmonized these passages, and hence seen to their "propriety" for his own epic. It is, however, the means of his adaptation and his variations on the original which warrant our
closest attention.

On several occasions Richard Heinze alluded to the possibility that Vergil might have been influenced in his imitation
of Homer by the observations of the ancient literary critics
which are now preserved in the scholia.[1] It is fitting, therefore,
that we begin our investigation with an examination of one of
the passages in which Heinze cites Aristarchus.

After Odysseus had found his way to the palace of Alcinous, he told the Phaeacians how he had arrived at Scheria, carefully concealing all reference to his identity and adventures prior to his stay at Ogygia (*Od.* VII. 241–97). He did not even reveal his name until the next day (IX. 19), despite the interrogations of his hosts. He had, of course, his reasons for secrecy. At the conclusion of his rather circumspect account, Odysseus gallantly apologized for Nausicaa because she did not personally bring him to the palace. Alcinous replied (309–15):

"Stranger, the inward heart in my breast is not of such a
kind
as to be recklessly angry. Always moderation is better.
O father Zeus, Athene and Apollo, how I wish
that, being the man you are and thinking the way that I do,
you could have my daughter and be called my son-in-law,
staying,
here with me. I would dower you with a house and prop-
erties,
if you stayed by your own good will . . ."

The scholiasts, citing Aristarchus, objected to Alcinous's offer on the grounds of its impropriety:

η 311: αἱ γάρ, ζεῦ πάτερ) τοὺς ἐξ Ἀρίσταρχος διστάζει Ὁμήρου εἶναι. εἰ δὲ καὶ Ὁμηρικοί, εἰκότως αὐτοὺς πε-ριαιρεθῆναί φησι. πῶς γὰρ ἀγνοῶν τὸν ἄνδρα μνηστεύεται αὐτῷ τὴν θυγατέρα καὶ οὐ προτρεπόμενος, ἀλλὰ λιπα-ρῶν; [P] ἄτοπος, φασίν, ἡ εὐχή · μὴ γὰρ ἐπιστάμενος ὅστις ἐστὶ μηδὲ πειραθεὶς εὔχεται σύμβιον αὐτὸν λαβεῖν καὶ γαμβρὸν ποιήσασθαι. ἦν μὲν παλαιὸν ἔθος τὸ προ-κρίνειν τοὺς ἀρίστους τῶν ξένων καὶ δι' ἀρετὴν ἐκδιδόναι τὰς θυγατέρας, ὡς καὶ ἐπὶ Βελλεροφόντου, Τυδέως, Πολυνείκους. . . . [T]²

O father Zeus) Aristarchus doubts that these six lines are Homer's. If Homeric [in appearance], he says that they might reasonably be removed. For how, when he does not know the man, [can] he espouse his daughter to him—not urging, but beseeching him?[P] The wish, they say, is unfitting, for neither knowing who he is nor making an attempt, he wishes to take him into his house and make him his son-in-law. It was, however, an ancient custom to select the no-blest of strangers and because of their excellence to give

them their daughters, as in the case of Bellerophon, Tydeus,
Polyneices. . . .[T]

At the very opening of *Aeneid* VII, Vergil begins to prepare the
way for the acceptability of Aeneas, also a stranger and foreigner,
as a suitor for Lavinia. Prior to the arrival of the Trojans,
omens had prevented Latinus from offering his daughter to any
of her suitors, including Turnus. The omens, in fact, had
enjoined him rather to keep her for a stranger destined yet to
come. This prophecy was no secret. Word of it had spread
throughout the Italian cities (VII. 58–106). We know that
Aeneas must marry Lavinia. He is, however, a stranger, and
as any Homeric scholar would know, the Alexandrians had
criticized as improper the offer of a princess in marriage to a
total stranger. The oracles serve primarily to reveal the divine
sanction for Lavinia's marriage to Aeneas, but at the same time
serve also to prepare for Latinus's ready awareness of the
Trojans and who they are, and for his offer of Lavinia to Aeneas
even before his appearance.

When the Trojan emissaries present themselves in court,
Latinus addresses them as follows (*Aen.* VII. 195 ff.):

"dicite, Dardanidae (neque enim nescimus et urbem
et genus, auditique advertitis aequore cursum),
quid petitis? . . ."

He continues to explain who the Latins are, and to add that
they know that Dardanus had left Italy to settle in Troy. The
Trojans reply that their leader Aeneas is also sprung from
Jupiter's line, and that they now wish to settle in Latium.
Vergil then adds that Latinus recalled the omens and oracle
and realized that Aeneas must be the stranger destined to marry
Lavinia. He welcomes the Trojans and asks that Aeneas come
to meet him. He continues (268 ff.):

"est mihi nata, viro gentis quam iungere nostrae
non patrio ex adyto sortes, non plurima caelo
monstra sinunt; generos externis adfore ab oris,
hoc Latio restare canunt, qui sanguine nostrum
nomen in astra ferant. hunc illum poscere fata
et reor et, si quid veri mens augurat, opto."

Servius's comment on this speech is especially noteworthy:

> 268: *est mihi nata*: male multi arguunt Vergilium
> quod Latinum induxit ultro filiam pollicentem,
> nec oraculum considerantes, quia Italo dari peni-
> tus non poterat, nec Aeneae meritum, quem decebat
> rogari. nam antiquis semper mos meliores generos
> rogare. . . .

This is precisely the point: the portents, oracle, and rumors had indeed gradually prepared the way for Aeneas's arrival and acceptance by Latinus.[3]

There are ample precedents for believing that Servius, or his source, and the critics to whom he refers had in mind the Alexandrian criticisms of Alcinous's wish from which Latinus's speech is drawn.[4] Servius was well aware that Vergil had taken all precautions against leaving himself vulnerable to the same charges made against Homer and that he had taken care to assure Aeneas's immediate acceptability as Lavinia's suitor. Indeed, it was so ordained by fate.

One of the most common grounds in antiquity for athetizing lines and whole passages of the *Iliad* and *Odyssey* was "impropriety": the line or lines in question were thought in some way to be offensive to refined taste in much the same way as Alcinous's prayer on behalf of his daughter was thought to be inappropriate. Modern scholars have frequently taken exception to such atheteses holding that the ancient commentators lacked a sense of "historical perspective" in condemning Homer in accordance with the social and religious mores of their own times.[5] Although it is true that with an increased awareness of the Homeric period and the nature of Homeric composition we are now in a better position to separate the wheat from the chaff of ancient criticism, we should not forget that authors in this period and following did write in conformity with the universally accepted Alexandrian and Pergamene critical canons and conventions and would have been disposed at least to consider the objections, if not to take them quite seriously. Vergil, in a sense as much a "court poet" as the Alexandrians, might well be expected to subscribe to the basic tenets concerning propriety, and certainly to have undertaken to avoid the grounds upon which such criticism was based.

The episode of Sarpedon's death is prefaced with a conversation between Zeus and Hera which concludes with Zeus resignedly accepting the fact that his son is inexorably doomed (*Il.* XVI. 431 ff.). A description of the furious battle follows with the death of Sarpedon, the healing of Glaucus by Apollo, and the struggle for Sarpedon's corpse. As the Greeks prevail and Sarpedon is despoiled of his armor, Homer returns us to Olympus. Zeus speaks (667–75):

> "Go if you will, beloved Phoibos, and rescue Sarpedon
> from under the weapons, wash the dark suffusion of blood
> from him,
> then carry him far away and wash him in a running river,
> anoint him in ambrosia, put ambrosial clothing upon him;
> then give him into the charge of swift messengers to carry
> him,
> of Sleep and Death, who are twin brothers, and those two
> shall lay him
> down presently within the rich countryside of broad Lykia
> where his brothers and countrymen shall give him due burial
> with tomb and gravestone. Such is the privilege of those
> who have perished."

Zenodotus athetized the entire passage on the grounds that it was not fitting for Apollo to tend to the corpse of Sarpedon since he is free from personal grief:

Π 667: εἰ δ' ἄγε νῦν) ἠθέτει Ζηνόδοτος · ἄτοπον γάρ
φησι τὸν ἀπενθῆ τοιαῦτα διακονεῖν. ἀλλὰ τοῦτο προστάσ-
σεται ὡς τιμώμενος ἐν Λυκίᾳ [T][6]

> "Go if you will. . .") Zenodotus athetized [this]. For he says
> that it is unfitting for one who is without grief to tend to
> such matters. But the order was given on the grounds that
> he [Apollo] is held in honor in Lycia.

Apollo, as the scholiast replied to Zenodotus's objection, is indeed honored in Lycia and might accordingly be considered deeply grieved at the death of a Trojan ally and Lycian.

Compared with this Homeric scene, the Vergilian parallel (*Aen.* XI. 532 ff.) is at once similar and dissimilar. After

Camilla has met with Turnus, the Rutulian forces station themselves for an ambush of the approaching Trojans. The scene
immediately shifts to the realm of the gods where Diana sadly
converses with Opis, one of her maidens. She tells the nymph
that Camilla's death is at hand and explains to her why the
maiden warrior is so dear to her: her father had dedicated her
in infancy to Diana and her life had always been a reflection
of the ways of the virgin goddess. Diana concludes by enjoining
Opis to descend to the scene of the battle and to exact vengeance upon Camilla's slayer. She concludes (593–94):

> "post ego nube cava miserandae corpus et arma
> inspoliata feram tumulo patriaeque reponam."

The narrative of the battle follows together with the *aristeia* and death of Camilla. Opis laments (841–47):

> "heu nimium, virgo, nimium crudele luisti
> supplicium Teucros conata lacessere bello!
> nec tibi desertae in dumis coluisse Dianam
> profuit aut nostras umero gessisse pharetras.
> non tamen indecorem tua te regina reliquit
> extrema iam in morte, neque hoc sine nomine letum
> per gentis erit aut famam patieris inultae...."

She thereupon slays Arruns.[7]

We should note that Vergil has omitted the morbid details
of the cleansing of the corpse, which as Leaf felt, may well lie
behind Zenodotus's athetesis. It is also noteworthy in the light
of the scholia that Diana will convey the corpse to a tomb in
its homeland. The long speech of Diana to Opis has made it
quite clear that the goddess is deeply grieved and concerned
that her beloved warrior-maiden receive a worthy burial. In
the Homeric episode the exact whereabouts of Apollo at the
death of Sarpedon was also called into question by Zenodotus.[8]
There can be no such question in the *Aeneid*: Diana states quite
clearly in her one speech what she intends to do and have done,
and the lament of Opis concludes the affair. Diana's commands
have been carried out, and we end as we began, on a note of
divine concern and involvement which serves as a frame for the
entire episode.[9] Vergil has also characteristically added that

Camilla's fame will not merely be celebrated in her own land
(as is the case with Sarpedon), but throughout whole nations.[10]
In short, led on by the Alexandrians' comments on decorum,
Vergil has developed the entire episode in such a manner as
to tighten the coherence of the action and so to heighten its
pathos.[11]

Let us turn now to several brief passages involving the
concern—or lack thereof—of the gods. The question here is
not so much of social or religious decorum but one rather of
literary propriety and effect.

The general dissimilarity in the treatment of the games in
honor of Patroclus (*Il.* XXIII) and those in memory of Anchises
(*Aen.* V) has often drawn comment and need not detain us here.[12]
The foot races in both epics are, however, similar in several respects and especially in that the outcome is suddenly changed
by the unexpected fall of one of the contestants. Near the
finish of the Homeric race, Odysseus trailing Ajax, utters a
prayer to Athena for aid (770–76):

"Hear me goddess; be kind; and come with strength for my
footsteps."
So he spoke in prayer, and Pallas Athene heard him.
She made his limbs light, both his feet and the hands above
them.
Now as they were for making their final sprint for the trophy,
there Aias slipped in his running, for Athene unbalanced him,
where dung was scattered on the ground from the bellowing
oxen slaughtered
by swift-footed Achilles, those he slew to honour Patroklos. . . .

The scholia comment that if Odysseus is granted renewed vigor,
then there is no need for Ajax to fall and *vice versa*:

Ψ 772 : . . . εἰ οὖν τὰ γυῖα ἐλαφρὰ ἐποίησεν, ἐνίκα ἂν
πάντως. πρὸς τί οὖν ἔτι τὸν Αἴαντα κατέβαλεν; [A]
περισσὸς ὁ στίχος καὶ λύων τὸ ἐναγώνιον · . . . ἄλλως
τε ἤρκει πρὸς τὴν νίκην τὸ πεσεῖν Αἴαντα · εἰ γὰρ τοῦτο ἦν, καὶ προειλήφει ἂν αὐτόν . . . . [T]

If, then, she had made his limbs lighter, he would be winning,
assuredly. Why, therefore, did she still overthrow Ajax?
[A] The line is superfluous [strange, or farfetched] and de-
stroys the competitiveness. . . . Above all, Ajax's falling

sufficed for his victory, for if this happened, he would
have gotten the advantage. . . . [T]

The criticism is rather insignificant, but it is noteworthy that
Vergil omitted reference to divine aid in his narrative of the
race, and Nisus slips purely by accident (V. 327 ff.). It should
be noted, however, that the scholiasts did regard the interest
of the gods as lending solemnity and distinction to the competition:

Ψ 383: κοτέσσατο *Φοῖβος*) σεμνοποιῆσαι πάλιν θέλων
τὸν ἀγῶνα καὶ θεοὺς συμφιλονεικοῦντας εἰσάγει. . . .
[BT]

Had not Phoibus been angry.) Again, wishing to solemnize
the games, he introduces the gods as being fond of engaging
together in rivalry. . . . [BT]

Vergil did resort to divine aid in his narrative of the ship race
(235 ff.), but what is far more significant, he employed omens
both before the games begin (84 ff.) and toward their conclusion
during the archery contest (485 ff.).

For the archery contest in the *Iliad*, Achilles ties a pigeon
to a mast and announces (855 ff.):

"Now let the man who hits the wild pigeon
take up and carry away home with him all the full axes.
But if one should miss the bird and still hit the string, that
man,
seeing that he is the loser, still shall have the half-axes."

Teucer and Meriones compete: the former misses the target
because, as Homer says, he failed to vow a hecatomb to Apollo,
but he does, however, sever the cord, which by accident frees
the bird. Heinze wrote that the feat, as a foreseen possibility,
is in itself a greater achievement than the one for which the
prize was offered.[13] The contest for the moment appeared over,
- but with a quick shot Meriones pierced the wing of the pigeon
as it flew skyward and the arrow returned to his feet as the
bird fluttered back to the mast where it died.

In the announcement of this contest in the *Aeneid*, Vergil omits reference to the possibility of hitting the cord, "perhaps," as Heinze remarked, "put on the track by the Homeric

criticism." The scholia had indeed noted the peculiarity of the conditions for the contest as set down by Achilles and had remarked that it would be better had they been omitted:

Ψ 855: ὃς μέν κε βάλῃ) . . . ἔδει δὲ μὴ προειπεῖν τὸ τῆς μηρίνθου ἀλλ' ὕστερον ὡς ἐναγώνιον συμβεβηκὸς εἰπεῖν. [T]

"Now let the man who hits") . . . he should not have fore-told the [possibility of hitting the] cord but [rather] given it later as having happened in the course of the contest.

Ψ 857: ὃς δέ κε μηρίνθοιο) . . . ὅτι βέλτιον ἦν τοῦτο μὴ προλέγεσθαι ὑπὸ Ἀχιλλέως ὥσπερ προγιγώσκοντος τὸ ἀπὸ τύχης συμβησόμενον. [A]

"But if one . . . hit the string") . . . this was better not foretold by Achilles as if he knew in advance what was about to happen by chance.

As the passage stands in the *Iliad*, it is as if the conditions were set forth with a knowledge of what actually is to happen.

Vergil recreates the event as follows (485 ff.): there are four contestants; the first misses the target completely but strikes the mast; the second also misses but severs the cord, and the pigeon soars into the air. Eurytion, who was prepared to shoot next, immediately brings down the bird as it soars overhead. The sequence is the result of the events, and if accidental and unexpected, is quite natural. This is what the ancient commentators on the Homeric scene had suggested would have been more appropriate.

The surprising conclusion of the archery contest in the *Iliad* was treated as a marvel, though not one of divine origin. As the bird falls from the mast, Homer adds (881):

And the people gazed upon it and wondered.

As we have already noted, however, the gods did take an interest in the games, and here, Apollo begrudged Teucer his shot because he failed to vow a hecatomb (865).[14] The scholia briefly comment:

Ψ 865: ἐπὶ εὐσέβειαν τοῦτο προτρέπει. [BT]

This prompts one to reverence.

With no target left for him, Acestes, the last of the competitors
in the Trojan games, simply shoots his arrow into the air where
it suddenly bursts into flames and vanishes like a shooting star
(*Aen.* V. 522–28). The Trojans, dumbstruck with awe, pray to
the gods and Aeneas accepts the portent. The games in the
Aeneid, solemnized by an omen as they began, are again so
honored by the gods at their conclusion.

The Homeric scholia frequently comment on the poet's use
of traditional epithets and descriptive adjectives especially when
for some reason or other they were considered inappropriate.[15]
Vergil does not employ such epithets nearly as often as Homer,
but when he does use them, it is with great care and attention
to their suitability. A case in point is his use of different names
for the goddess Minerva; Pallas and Tritonia.

In the first instance in the *Aeneid*, Juno refers to her as
Pallas, as she recalls her destruction of the Greek fleet after
the sack of Troy with the thunderbolts of Jupiter (I. 39 f.).
Servius provides us with the traditional significance of the name
(*ad Aen.* I. 39):

> Pallasne: Minerva ἀπὸ τοῦ πάλλειν τὸ δόρυ,
> id est, ab hastae concussione; vel quod Pallantem gi-
> ganta occiderit.

Fraenkel, in demonstrating Servius's dependency upon the
Greek scholia, refers to AB on *Iliad* I. 200:

> Παλλάδα τὴν Ἀθηνᾶν ἐπιθετικῶς, ἤτοι ἀπὸ τοῦ πάλλειν
> καὶ κραδαίνειν τὸ δόρυ (πολεμικὴ γὰρ ἡ θεός), ἢ ὅτι
> Πάλλαντα ἕνα τῶν γιγάντων ἀπέκτεινεν, ἢ ἀπὸ τοῦ ἀνα-
> παλθῆναι αὐτὴν ἀπὸ τῆς κεφαλῆς τοῦ Διός. . . .

> Pallas, the epithet of Athena either from brandishing [*pallein*]
> and waving her spear (for she is a warlike goddess), or because
> she slew Pallas, one of the giants, or from the fact that she
> was sprung from the head of Zeus. . . .

He continues, "Schol. 'V' to *Od.* I. 252 says much the same in
a more abbreviated form. It is, as will be noted, word for word
the same as the reading in Servius's commentary":[16]

> Πάλλας) ἐπιθετικῶς ἡ Ἀθηνᾶ, ἀπὸ τοῦ πάλλειν τὸ δόρυ ·
> ἢ ὅτι Πάλλαντα ἀνεῖλεν, ἕνα τῶν γιγάντων.

Pallas) Athena's epithet from brandishing her spear, or because she destroyed Pallas, one of the giants.

As the hurler of Jupiter's thunderbolts, Minerva is aptly called Pallas, as *Pallas Fulminatrix*.[17] The first reference to Minerva as Tritonia comes in Sinon's speech where again the goddess is directly involved in war as an active agent. Sinon is telling the Trojans how Ulysses and Diomedes had violated the sanctity of the Palladium (*Aen*. II. 169 ff.):

> ex illo fluere ac retro sublapsa referri
> spes Danaum, fractae vires, aversa deae mens.
> nec dubiis ea signa dedit Tritonia monstris.
> vix positum castris simulacrum: arsere coruscae
> luminibus flammae arrectis, salsusque per artus
> sudor iit, terque ipsa solo (mirabile dictu)
> emicuit parmamque ferens hastamque trementem.

Sinon continues to tell the Trojans that Calchas had recommended that the Greeks escape by sea after they have atoned for the profanation by erecting the effigy of the horse. Servius comments (*ad Aen*. II. 171):

> Tritonia: aut quasi terribilis, ἀπὸ τοῦ τρεῖν, id est, "timere," aut a Tritone amne Boeotiae, aut a Tritonide palude Africae, iuxta quam nata dicitur.

Fraenkel once more points to the scholia as also reflecting the source of Servius's remark, for example, AD on Θ 39:

> Τριτογένεια) "Ομηρος μὲν τὴν τὸ τρεῖν καὶ ["i.e."] εὐλα-
> βεῖσθαι γεννῶσαν τοῖς ἀνθρώποις (πολεμικὴ γὰρ ἡ θεός),
> οἱ δὲ νεώτεροί φασι τὴν παρὰ τῷ Τρίτωνι ποταμῷ γεννη-
> θεῖσαν, ὅς ἐστι τῆς Λιβύης.

and Δ 515:[18]

> Τριτογένεια) ἡ 'Αθηνᾶ ἡ τὸ τρεῖν καὶ φοβεῖσθαι γεννῶσα
> τοῖς πολεμίοις, ἢ ἐπὶ Τρίτωνι ποταμῷ. . . .

Tritogeneia) Homer [says?] that she [is the one] begetting fear in men, that is to say [causing them] to take precautions (for the goddess is warlike), but the more recent [scholars] say that she was born by the Triton River, which is in Libya. Δ 515: Athena, who begets fear and terror in her enemies, . . .

Here again the variant name for Athena has exactly the significance appropriate to the situation: the Greeks do indeed, as we are to believe, at least, become terrified at the awesome behavior of the *simulacrum* and take precautions for their safety (II. 176 ff.).

The goddess is referred to again in the Laocoon episode. After the serpents had destroyed the seer and his sons, Aeneas says (*Aen.* II. 225–29):

> "at gemini lapsu delubra ad summa dracones
> effugiunt saevaeque petunt Tritonidis arcem,
> sub pedibusque deae clipeique sub orbe teguntur.
> tum vero tremefacta novus per pectora cunctis
> insinuat pavor. . . ."

The emphasis is on the *novus pavor*, the terror that creeps into the hearts of the Trojans. Aeneas continues to tell Dido that the Trojans believed that Laocoon had paid for his crime and that they immediately began to drag the horse into the city.

In each of the instances discussed above it appears as though Vergil has employed the name which, according to the traditional etymology and implication of the root, was most suitable to the situation.[19] Servius's interpretations, while they seem at first sight somewhat irrelevant and fanciful, may well be a faithful and accurate reflection of Vergil's reasoning in his choice of particular names at the particular moment. There can be no question of whether or not Vergil knew the scholia: the point, however, is that like Servius, Vergil seems well acquainted with the traditional interpretations of the various epithets used for Athena.[20]

The most obvious use that Vergil might have made of the commentaries on Homer would have been for aid in translating specific words and phrases that were obscure. We have already seen that Livius Andronicus might well have used the commentaries in this way, but such instances are extremely difficult to demonstrate for no one could presume to say when Vergil used a "lexicon," much less, what "edition."[21] Nonetheless, some glosses on the *Iliad* are quite detailed and seem to preserve full discussions giving us several possible meanings of the words in question, not unlike the scholia on Athena's epithets. In such cases as these, Vergil would either have to exercise his own judgment in the matter or simply employ the several conjectures in his adaptation. In the latter case, we might with some certainty assume that Vergil had knowledge of the particular gloss.

R. S. Conway has pointed to several passages in the *Aeneid* in which Vergil has expanded the Homeric versions for no apparent reason.[22] In at least one instance the expansion may well have resulted from the fact that Vergil had incorporated the gloss as well as the questionable Greek word into his version. During the fighting in *Aeneid* VII, the following description occurs (535–39):

> corpora multa virum circa seniorque Galaesus,
> dum paci medium se offert, iustissimus unus
> qui fuit Ausoniisque olim ditissimus arvis:
> quinque greges illi balantum, quina redibant
> armenta, et terram centum vertebat aratris.

Conway conjectured that lines 538–39 were an expansion of the words πολυκτήμων πολυλήϊος which are part of a brief description of a man Telamonian Ajax slays (*Il.* V. 612–14):

> and [he] struck Amphios, Selagos's son, who *rich in pos-*
> *sessions*
> and *rich in cornland* had lived in Paisos, but his own destiny
> brought him companion in arms to Priam. . . .

The gloss on the latter word explains it as meaning one who has many fields or many herds as opposed to meaning one who has "much booty" from war or pillaging:

> *E* 613: πολυλήϊος) πολλὰ λήϊα ἔχων ἢ πολλὰ θρέμματα
> ἔχων, πολυθρέμμων. λεία δὲ λέγεται καὶ τὰ ἐκ πολέμου
> λάφυρα ἢ τὰ ἀπὸ λῃζείας. [D]

Vergil has simply particularized the herds, which are not mentioned by Homer, and given the "exact" extent of Galaesus's fields. The reason for the expansion of the two Homeric words becomes obvious: by incorporating the full meaning of the word as given in the gloss, Vergil, in characteristic fashion, has increased the pathos of an already pathetic scene.

Such personal details of a warrior's life are common in Homer, and at times occur even when opponents address each other in the heat of battle. In one such encounter, Achilles slays Iphition. As the warrior falls, Achilles vaunts over him (*Il.* XX. 389–92):

> "Lie there, Otrynteus' son, most terrifying of all men.
> Here is your death, but your generation was by the lake
> waters
> of Gyge, where is the allotted land of your fathers
> by fish-swarming Hyllos and the whirling waters of Hermos."

This address, with its genealogical details, is reminiscent of many in the *Iliad.* The scholiasts clearly objecting to the use of these details comment:[23]

> Υ 389: κεῖσαι, 'Οτρυντεΐδη) ὅτι ὁ Αχιλλεὺς γιγνώσκων
> αὐτὸν ἐξ ὀνόματος καλεῖ. [A]

> "Lie there, Otrynteus' son.") [Note?] that Achilles, knowing him, calls him by name.

A similar criticism is made against Diomedes' knowledge of Dolon's name after their encounter in the darkness of the battlefield (*Il.* X. 447), for Dolon had at no time revealed his identity. There, however, the scholia add that it is more than likely that after nine years of fighting, the warriors would know one another's names, and especially since Dolon is the son of a rich herald (A on K 447). There is a considerable difference between a warrior's knowledge of his adversary's name and his knowledge of his lineage and homeland, including the details of his place of birth. As petty as this criticism may be, the peculiarity was noted by the ancient commentators as being out of place in the circumstance.

There is a similar "epitaph" pronounced over a fallen warrior in the *Aeneid,* but the address comes not from the mouth of the victor; rather, as was the case with Galaesus, it is pronounced by the poet himself (*Aen.* XII. 542–47):

> te quoque Laurentes viderunt, Aeole, campi
> oppetere et late terram consternere tergo:
> occidis, Argivae quem non potuere phalanges
> sternere nec Priami regnorum eversor Achilles;

hic tibi mortis erant metae, domus alta sub Ida,
Lyrnesi domus alta, solo Laurente sepulchrum.

Here, as the words of the poet, the details, far from being out of place, serve to heighten the pathos.

It is also noteworthy that Vergil has inverted the order of the sites as they occur in Achilles' boast and has thereby secured a still more poignant and epigrammatic effect. Weariness and endless toil are suggested by the fighting over the many years and in the two wars. Furthermore, the mention of the Greeks and Achilles brings out the futility of his having survived combat with the greatest of heroes only to be killed at last far from his beloved homeland in this strange and hostile region.

There are many such instances like the preceding in which Vergil has taken lines or passages from Homer which were criticized for some reason by the ancient commentators and used them to full advantage in a different context.[24] The reason need not have been that Vergil was so much in agreement with the particular criticisms but rather that he realized the intrinsic effectiveness of the Homeric passages especially when adapted in a more suitable context.

After she has exhorted Diomedes to attack Ares, Athena thrusts Sthenelus from the chariot and takes up the reins herself (*Il.* V. 837–39):

> and she herself, a goddess in her anger, stepped into the
> chariot
> beside brilliant Diomedes, and the oaken axle groaned aloud
> under the weight, carrying a dread goddess and a great man.

The last two lines were athetized on the grounds that they were unnecessary and unfitting (paradoxical); the fact that the pair are described as "dread" and "great" ("noblest") does not necessarily mean that they are "heavier." Perhaps also, the scholiast felt that there was a certain "indelicacy" in calling attention to weight.

E 838–39: ἀθετοῦνται στίχοι δύο, ὅτι οὐκ ἀναγκαῖοι καὶ γελοῖοι καί τι ἐναντίον ἔχοντες. τί γάρ, εἰ χείριστοι ἦσαν ταῖς ψυχαῖς, εὐειδεῖς δὲ καὶ εὔσαρκοι; [A]

The two lines are athetized because they are not necessary
and are paradoxical [ridiculous] and have somewhat the
opposite [effect]. What, then, if they were most inferior
as persons [lit., in their souls], but well-shaped and fleshy?

Nevertheless, these lines have rightly been admired, and it has
been objected in turn that the grammarian seems to have forgotten, or been unaware of the "naive point of view of Homeric
poetry" in his remark.[25]

Vergil adapted this passage in a similar situation: Juturna
assumes the form of Metiscus, Turnus's charioteer, and drives
off leading her brother away from the path of Aeneas (*Aen.*
XII. 468 ff.). The lines that were athetized have been omitted,
though for different reasons. Juturna, disguised as Metiscus,
can hardly be compared with the "dread Athena" armed for
battle. Still, the athetized lines were admired by Vergil who
turned them to yet greater advantage in a far different context.
When Charon saw the Sibyl with the golden bough on the shore
of the Stygian waters, he turned the stern of his bark toward
them (VI. 411–14):

inde alias *animas*, quae per iuga longa sedebant,
deturbat laxatque foros; simul accipit alveo
ingentem Aenean. gemuit sub pondere cumba
sutilis et multam accepit rimosa paludem.

The contrast between the gigantic Aeneas and the formless,
insubstantial souls of the dead is indeed both eerie and "grotesque."[26]

It is not so much a matter of whether or not Vergil had
agreed with the athetesis of the couplet for he clearly admired
the lines and the effect for which Homer had intended them.
What is equally obvious from the use of this passage is the
fact that Vergil was sensitive to the most minute of poetic
details and that he seems to have treasured them and used them
where they would be most fitting and effective for his own
artistic purposes. The following conflation of Homeric lines
would tend to substantiate this still more.

When Diomedes kills the sleeping Rhesus, Homer tells us
that the Thracian was breathing heavily (*Il.* X. 494–97):

But when the son of Tydeus came to the king, and this was
the thirteenth man, he stripped the sweetness of life from
him
as he lay heavily breathing—since a bad dream stood by his
head
in the night. . . .—Oineus' son, by the device of Athene.[27]

The last line was athetized by Aristarchus and did not appear
in the texts of either Zenodotus or Aristophanes, presumably
because Rhesus could not know Diomedes and therefore could
not dream about him. Whatever the reason, it does seem odd
that Athena would send him such a dream, since she is protecting
Diomedes and Odysseus.[28] The scholium reads in full:

K 497: ἀθετεῖται, ὅτι καὶ τῇ συνθέσει εὐτελής · καὶ μὴ
ῥηθέντος δὲ νοεῖται ὅτι ὡς ὄναρ ἐφίσταται τῷ ʿΡήσῳ
ὁ Διομήδης. καὶ τὸ διὰ μῆτιν ᾿Αθηνῆς λυπεῖ · μᾶλλον
γὰρ διὰ τὴν Δόλωνος ἀπαγγελίαν. οὔτε ἐν τῇ Ζηνοδότου
οὔτε ἐν τῇ ᾿Αριστοφάνους ἐφέρετο. [A][29]

The line is athetized because it is meaningless [lit., worth-
less] in its context; and though it is not stated, it is to be
understood that Diomedes stands like a dream over Rhesus.
The phrase, "by the device of Athena," moreover, is vexing;
rather it [his standing there] is the result of Dolon's report.
The line was not transmitted in the editions of either Zenodotus or Aristophanes.

Whether or not the line in question was a later interpolation
need not detain us, but as Leaf has pointed out: "The idea seems
to be that Rhesus is breathing heavily under the influence of
an ominous dream which has actually appeared to him, but
fails to save him." This is clear with or without the line.

Vergil also appears to have known and even agreed with
the discussion concerning the line, for he adapts the passage
for use in exactly the same situation, but without the athetized
words. While Nisus and Euryalus are creeping through the camp
of the slumbering Latins and slaying all who lie in their path,
Nisus comes upon Rhamnes, breathing heavily in his sleep, even
as Rhesus was (IX. 325–28):

Rhamnetem adgreditur, qui forte tapetibus altis
exstructus toto proflabat pectore somnum,

rex idem et regi Turno gratissimus augur,
sed non augurio potuit depellere pestem.

Vergil, though omitting the dream, has made the victim an
augur who might have known his fate in advance, but ironic-
ally did not. The same effect that was intended by the Homeric
lines has been achieved while the grounds of the objection to
the line in the *Iliad* have been removed. Curiously enough, the
line that Vergil has substituted also comes from the *Iliad*. In
the "Catalogue of Ships" Homer lists among the Mysians the
augur Ennomus (II. 858–60):

> Chromis, with Ennomus the augur, was lord of the Mysians;
> yet his reading of birds could not keep off dark destruction
> but he went down under the hands of swift-running Aia-
> kides. . . .[30]

The reason for Vergil's substitution of one Homeric line for
another would seem not so much the result of "poetic integration," or a "subconscious" fusion of similar ideas, but rather
an extremely conscious attempt to improve and refine the
passages which he has adapted.[31] Here as elsewhere in his effort to maintain the "epic illusion," Vergil has "improved upon
Homer" with Homer.

While discussing the view that Vergil did not simply imitate Homeric similes in a "thoughtless, mechanical fashion,"
Heinze cites the following pair of similes and indicates how
Vergil achieved a more effective use of his adaptation by a
change in context. Heinze's comment is well taken, but the
context is not all Vergil has changed.[32]

After Hector had chided him for his idleness (*Il.* VI.
315–41), Paris donned his armor (505 ff.):

> he ran in confidence of his quick feet through the city.
> As when some stalled horse who has been corn-fed at the
>   manger
> breaking free of his rope gallops over the plain in thunder
> to his accustomed bathing place in a sweet-running river
> and in the pride of his strength holds high his head, and
>   the mane floats
> over his shoulders; sure of his glorious strength, the quick
>   knees

carry him to the beloved places and the pasture of horses;
so from uttermost Pergamos came Paris, the son of
Priam, shining in all his armor of war as the sun shines,
laughing aloud, and his quick feet carried him. . . .

He overtook Hector and said to him (815 f.):

"Brother, I fear that I have held back your haste, by being
slow on the way, not coming in time, as you commanded me."

The context of the Vergilian simile is as follows: while the
Latins are discussing the question of war or peace with the
Trojans, Drances rebukes Turnus, who in an angry reply, con-
sents, indeed, welcomes the challenge to fight Aeneas in hand
to hand combat. News is suddenly brought that the Trojans in
full battle array are approaching the city. Turnus at once
orders the Latin army to march out and confront them (*Aen.*
XI. 486–97):

cingitur ipse furens certatim in proelia Turnus.
iamque adeo rutilum thoraca indutus aënis
horrebat squamis surasque incluserat auro,
tempora nudus adhuc, laterique accinxerat ensem,
fulgebatque alta decurrens aureus arce
exsultatque animis et spe iam praecipit hostem;
qualis ubi abruptis fugit praesepia vinclis
tandem liber equus, campoque potitus aperto
aut ille in pastus armentaque tendit equarum
aut adsuetus aquae perfundi flumine noto
emicat, arrectisque fremit cervicibus alte
luxurians luduntque iubae per colla, per armos.

Vergil's adaptation of the simile omits reference to the stallion's
being "corn-fed" (lit., full-fed), which was included in Ennius's
version; on the other hand, Vergil has also strongly emphasized
the exuberance of his freedom.[33]

It is noteworthy that it is precisely with the Homeric
phrase "full-fed" that the Hellenistic scholars wrestled: the word
ἀκοστήσας is a *hapax legomenon* whose meaning was contested,
whether from ἄκος, meaning cure, ἀκοστή, meaning grain or
barley, or ἄχος, meaning pain or distress, and in this latter
sense the participle would therefore mean "unable to endure the
confinement of the stable":

Z 506: ἀκοστήσας) ἄκος τῆς στάσεως λαβὼν, τουτέστιν ἴα-
μα, καὶ κριθιάσας. κυρίως δὲ πᾶσαι αἱ τροφαὶ ἀκοσταὶ
καλοῦνται παρὰ Θεσσαλοῖς, ὡς καὶ Νίκανδρος, παρὰ τὸ
ἵστασθαι τὰ σώματα τρεφόμενα. ἐν ἄλλῳ, καιρῷ παρα-
λαβών. βέλτιον δὲ, δυσχεράνας ἐπὶ τῇ τῆς φάτνης στά-
σει. ... [AT]
ἡ δὲ διπλῆ πρὸς τὸ ἀκοστήσας, ὅτι ἄλλοι ἄλλως ἀπέδω-
καν · ἔστι δὲ ἤτοι ἐν ἄχει γενόμενος διὰ τὴν στάσιν, ἢ
ἄκος τι καὶ βοήθημα τῆς στάσεως ζητῶν. [A][34]

Having taken a cure for his standing stationary, that is, a
medicine, indeed since he suffered from "krithiasis" [a sur-
feit caused by overfeeding with barley]. Grain of all kinds
is regularly called "barley" by the Thessalians, and Nicander,
too, from the fact that their bodies stand while being fed.
Elsewhere [or, in another interpretation], having gotten its
meaning from the context. But it is better [taking it to
mean] unable to endure his confinement at the manger. ...
[AT] Note the word "full-fed," how it is rendered in various ways by various critics; it means either being in distress
from his stationary position or seeking some cure or remedy
for it. [A]

The scholiasts also debated the meaning of the word which
Archilochus and the *neôteroi* took as "being eager," whereas
others, and apparently more correctly, took it as meaning
"galloping" (so, too, Lattimore):

Z 507: πεδίοιο) ἡ διπλῆ, ὅτι ἐλλείπει ἡ "δία," καὶ τὸ
"κροαίνων" οὐκ ἔστιν "ἐπιθυμῶν," ὡς Ἀρχίλοχος ἐξέ-
λαβεν, ἀλλ' "ἐπικροτῶν" τοῖς ποσὶ διὰ τοῦ πεδίου. [A]
ἄλλως. οἱ νεώτεροι "ἐπιθυμεῖν" τὸ "κροαίνειν," καὶ Ἀρχίλοχος. [A]

the plain) Note that he has omitted the preposition "over"
with the word "plain" and that the word *kroainôn* does not
mean "being eager" [or "yearning for"], as Archilochus took
it, but "clattering," that is, with his hoofs over the plain. [A]
Archilochus and the *neôteroi* took *kroainôn* to mean "being
eager." [A]

Finally, there are comments on the horse's mane, which was
taken to be a source of his pride and befitting the handsome
appearance of Paris. And so the comparison, then, includes
pride and arrogance, and an "irrational arrogance" at that:

Z 509: χαῖται) δοκεῖ ἡ κόμη μεγαλοπρεπείας αἰτία εἶναι
τοῖς ἵπποις. [AT] καὶ Πάρις δὲ εὔκομος. πρεπόντως δὲ
τοῦτο ἐπὶ τοῦ καλλωπιστοῦ· καὶ τὸ παράδειγμα ἀπὸ
γαυρικοῦ ἵππου καὶ ἀλογίστου. [B]

Mane: It seems that the mane is a cause [occasion] for the
magnificence in horses [AT]. And Paris had beautiful hair.
This, then, is fittingly [added] for one who pays attention
to his appearance; the point of comparison is [taken] from
a haughty [arrogant] and irrational horse. [B]

Still more was said of this simile which seems to have been
admired as much in antiquity as it has been in modern times.
The same unaltered simile occurs again in the *Iliad* to describe
Hector as he leaps up, miraculously healed by Apollo, and ex-
horts the Trojans to renew the battle (XV. 262 ff.):

He (Apollo) spoke, and breathed huge strength into the
shepherd of the people.
As when some stalled horse who has been corn-fed at the
manger
breaking free of his rope gallops over the plain in thunder.
. . . .
so Hector moving rapidly his feet and knees went onward,
stirring the horsemen when he heard the god's voice speak.

The four lines of the original simile (omitted above) were athetized by Aristarchus on the grounds that they are more suitable
for Paris because of the comeliness of his appearance and
because the reference to the "stall" is more in keeping with
his dalliance in Helen's bedchamber.[35] The simile here emphasizes the speed with which Hector springs up, whereas in its
first use, a second scholium adds, it represents Paris's "elation":

O 265: εἰωθὼς λούεσθαι) ἀπὸ τούτου ἕως τοῦ "ῥίμφα ἑ
γοῦνα φέρει" (268) ἀθετοῦνται στίχοι δ', καὶ ἀστερίσκοι
παράκεινται, ὅτι οἰκειότερον ἐπ' Ἀλεξάνδρου (*Il.* VI,
508). καὶ τὸ τῆς καλλονῆς καὶ τὸ τῆς ὅλης μορφῆς καὶ
τὸ τῆς στάσεως τοῦ ἵππου πρὸς τὸν ἐν θαλάμῳ διατετρι-
φότα ἀντιπαράκειται, ἥ τε κατὰ τὴν αἰφνίδιον ἐξόρμησιν
ὁμοιότης. καὶ τὸ "κυδιόων, ὑψοῦ δὲ κάρη ἔχει" ἐφ' Ἕκτορος τοῦ ἀρτίως ἑαυτὸν ἀνιστῶντος ἐκ τῆς λιποθυμίας οὐχ
ἁρμόζει. τοὺς μέντοι προκειμένους τῶν ἠθετημένων δύο
στίχους δεῖ μένειν, πρὸς οὓς καὶ ἡ ἀνταπόδοσις γίνεται. [A]
O 268: ἡ παραβολὴ διὰ τὸ τάχος, ἡ δὲ τοῦ Πάριδος διὰ
τὴν ἔπαρσιν. [V]

"Accustomed bathing place") The four lines from here to
"his quick knees carry him" (268) are athetized and one
notes that they are more suitable for Paris (*Il.* VI. 508),
for the allusion to beauty and whole appearance and stationary position of the stallion correspond to the one who
has passed time in a bedchamber, and the likeness is for
the sudden rushing forth. The phrase "in the pride of his
strength" [lit., "bear himself proudly"], "holds high his head"
does not fit Hector who has just now recovered himself
from unconsciousness. The two lines preceding the athetesis should remain since they correspond to the point
of comparison.

O 268: The comparison is based upon the idea of speed, but
the one concerning Paris is based on his "elation."

This sizable and imaginative bulk of commentary allows us
some idea of the care that the Alexandrians expended on poetic
diction in addition to the fine points of grammar and textual
criticism—a care very similar to the meticulous precision which
Vergil exhibits in his use of Homeric materials. The simile as
a whole does appear more suitable for Paris than for Hector,
even as with Vergil's modifications, it becomes still more appropriate for Turnus, and especially his psychological state.

We have already noted that Vergil has omitted reference
to the detail that the stallion was "full-fed" and has instead
emphasized its newly acquired freedom (*tandem liber*, l. 493).
This implies that the stallion had for some time been trying to
escape his confinement, which was naturally a source of annoy-
ance and restiveness. This is exactly the meaning which one
school of ancient thought had given the participle ἀκοστήσας
equating it with ἄχος and δυσχεραίνω; they felt it was "better"
than "full-fed" (Z 506 A). Turnus's angry remarks in the assembly surely indicate that he was more than "elated" (O 268 V)
and "eager" (Z 507 A) to escape the confines and inactivity of
the debate and to storm off to battle.

Archilochus and the *neôteroi*, previously noted, took κροαί-
νω to mean ἐπιθυμέω, "eager," although the word would more
logically seem to mean "gallop," as was accepted in antiquity.
It is, however, clear that the scholiasts were attempting to
see in the word an additional attempt of the poet to stress the

jubilant emotions of the stallion as he gallops "yearning for the plain." This would account for the genitive πεδίοιο, as well, and would be less redundant with the verb, θείη, which Vergil has translated as *fugit*.

It is also interesting to note how Philostratus made use of this word in late antiquity. Far from meaning "gallop," κροαίνειν as a metaphor appears to mean "luxuriate," "wanton" (*LSJ*, *s.v.*), and was used to describe a rhetorician (*Im.* I. 30). Oddly enough, this is exactly what Vergil says of the stallion at the close of his simile (496–97):

> emicat, arrectisque fremit cervicibus alte
> *luxurians* luduntque iubae per colla, per armos.

The neighing is also an addition to the Homeric simile and is quite in keeping with the description of the fiery stallion as it tosses its mane, clearly indicative of its own, and by analogy, of Turnus's pride in himself and in his appearance. This is precisely the view of the scholiasts on the Homeric simile (Z 509 B).[36]

There are many comments in the scholia which concern the effectiveness of Homer's narrative skills; one, for example, is his method of portraying the reaction of those who are witness to the event which is being described.[37] Even when Homer does not explicitly portray the effect on the bystanders, at times the scholiasts felt that this was implied in the descriptive details. At the opening of his *aristeia* in *Iliad* V, Diomedes is described as follows (1–8):

> There to Tydeus's son, Diomedes, Pallas Athene
> granted strength and daring, that he might be conspicuous
> among all the Argives and win the glory of valour.
> She made weariless fire blaze from his shield and helmet
> like that star of the waning summer who beyond all stars
> rises bathed in the ocean stream to glitter in brilliance.
> Such was the fire she made blaze from his head and shoulders
> and urged him into the middle of the fighting, where most
>   were struggling.

Although Zoilus had ridiculed these lines on the grounds that Diomedes would thus run the risk of being "totally consumed," other commentators regarded the fire/gleam on his weapons as having the purpose of making him all the more terrifying to the Trojans. Homer, moreover, used fire as a representation of the intensity and fervor of warriors' emotions in battle:[38]

E 4: δαῖέ οἱ) ἀντὶ τοῦ φαντασίαν πυρὸς ἀπὸ τῶν ὅπλων αὐτοῦ ἐποίει φαίνεσθαι, ὥστε πλέον εἶναι αὐτὸν ἐπίφοβον τοῖς Τρωσίν. [A]

Fire to blaze) Rather than [using] imagery of fire, he makes it [actually] appear from his weapons with the result that he is the more terrifying to the Trojans.

E 7: (Zoilus's comment) . . . ἂν καταφλεχθῆναι ὁ ἥρως. ἔνιοι μὲν οὖν παραλελεῖφθαι [παρειλῆφθαι?] τὸ ὡς κατὰ συνήθειαν τῷ ποιητῇ, ὡς καὶ ἐν ἑτέροις · "ὣς οἱ μέν μάρναντο δέμας πυρός ·" (*Il.* XVIII, 1) καὶ ἐνθάδε τὸ "δαῖέ οἱ ἀκάματον πῦρ," ἵν᾽ ᾖ ὡς πυρὸς φαντασία, οὐκ εἰδικῶς πῦρ. [A]

. . . the hero would have been totally consumed. Some say, at all events, that this must be passed over [taken as in keeping with?] on the grounds that it is in keeping with the poet's stylistic usage, as in other [passages]: "So they fought on in the likeness of blazing fire." (Il. XVIII. 1); so here, the words "made weariless fire blaze," so that it is fire as imagery [poetic imagination], not fire specifically.

E 7: πῦρ δαῖεν ἀπὸ κρατός). . . . λύεται δὲ καὶ ἐκ τῆς λέξεως διχῶς, ἢ ὅτι τὸ πῦρ οὐ κυριολογεῖ, ἀλλ᾽ ἐπὶ τῆς λαμπηδόνος τίθησιν ἢ ὅτι μετωνυμικῶς ἀπὸ κρατός τε καὶ ὤμων λέγει . . . ἢ καὶ τοῦ ἔθους · εἴωθε γὰρ ἐπὶ τῶν μαχομένων τὸ πῦρ λαμβάνειν εἰς παράστασιν τῆς συντόνου καὶ ἐνθέρμου ὁρμῆς [cf. *Il.* IV. 342 and XI. 596]. . . . [B]

Fire blazed from his head . . .) [The difficulty] is resolved in two ways from [considerations of] style, either that he does not mean fire literally but intends it for the brilliance [gleaming of his armor] or that he says "from his head and shoulders" by way of metonymy. . . or [secondly] from his usual device; for he was accustomed to use fire in battle scenes as a representation of an intense and fiery struggle.

The scholiasts also attempted to identify the star as Sirius, which is fairly obvious from the reference to summer. Sirius, it should be noted, appears in another simile used to describe Achilles as he rushes towards the walls of Troy (*Il.* XXII. 25–32):

> The aged Priam was the first of all whose eyes saw him
> as he swept across the flat land in full shining, like that star
> which comes on in the autumn and whose conspicuous
> brightness
> far outshines the stars that are numbered in the night's
> darkening,
> the star they give the name of Orion's Dog, which is brightest
> among the stars, and yet is wrought as a sign of evil
> and brings on the great fever for unfortunate mortals.
> Such was the flare of the bronze that girt his chest in his
> running.
> The old man groaned aloud. . . .

Here, as the scholiasts noted, the meaning is quite clear: the simile points to the impending doom of Hector.

Vergil seems to have taken both these similes and fused them together in his description of Aeneas as he arrives during the battle around the Trojan camp. He raises his shield into the rays of the sun as a signal to his beleaguered men who fight now with a renewed courage. Vergil continues (*Aen.* X. 267–77):

> at Rutulo regi ducibusque ea mira videri
> Ausoniis, donec versas ad litora puppis
> respiciunt totumque adlabi classibus aequor.
> ardet apex capiti cristisque a vertice flamma
> funditur et vastos umbo vomit aureus ignis:
> non secus ac liquida si quando nocte cometae
> sanguinei lugubre rubent, aut Sirius ardor
> ille sitim morbosque ferens mortalibus aegris
> nascitur et laevo contristat lumine caelum.
>   Haud tamen audaci Turno fiducia cessit
> litora praecipere et venientis pellere terra.

Turnus then encourages his men with a brief exhortation. The description is presented not only for its visual appearance, but as well for its effect upon the Ausonians, as indeed Heinze has pointed out.[39] The Servian commentary also appears to have seen the whole passage in this light, as the comment on the metaphor, *adlabi*, seems to indicate (*ad Aen.* X. 269):

adlabi classibus aequor: . . . aut aequore classem labi. qui-
dam ita exponunt, ut hoc ad phantasiam Rutulorum refe-
rant, quoniam admirantibus his unde tanta fiducia animos
Troianorum incessisset, repentina facies multarum navium
adpropinquantium perinde visa est, atque si ipsum aequor
cum classibus allaberetur.[40]

Vergil, doubtlessly intending less to avoid the difficulties raised
by Zoilus on the description of Diomedes, but fully aware of
the interpretations of the scholia, nevertheless has omitted the
line which refers to the fire blazing about the head and shoulders
of the Homeric hero (*Il.* V. 7) and added the details of the
Sirius simile which was used to describe Achilles (*Aen.* X. 272 f.).
As a result he has made explicit the symbolism which the scholiasts had felt was implied in the Diomedes passage with its
reference to the "star of the waning summer," and has used
the description as a whole to portray both the actual appearance
of Aeneas as well as the reactions of the Rutulians when they
suddenly become aware of his arrival.[41] This is again exactly
the purpose which the scholiasts saw in Homer's description of
the fire blazing from the armor of Diomedes.

On several occasions Knauer raises the question of the
possible relationship of the allegorical interpretations of the
scholia to Vergil's understanding of Homer.[42] He cites as a
possible example the song of Iopas after Dido's banquet at the
close of *Aeneid* I and calls attention to the allegorical interpretations of the scholia on the Ares-Aphrodite tale as sung by
Demodocus while the Phaeacians were feasting Odysseus.
There the tale was allegorized as a cosmological exposition of
the universe—a *de rerum Natura* in miniature. Even as the
scholiasts found the amorous activities of the gods unfitting and
allegorized the passage, so, as Servius realized, it was quite
proper for Vergil to have the bard sing openly of the "nature
of the universe" in the court of a "chaste" queen.[43] Be that
as it may, there is one allegorization of a Homeric passage
which Vergil seems to have turned to good use in the *Aeneid*.

The shield of Achilles has been referred to as a "metaphor
of the whole heroic world."[44] Crates and his followers, we are

told by Eustathius, regarded the shield of Agamemnon as an "imitation of the cosmos"; the shield of Achilles, moreover, also when allegorized, was seen to reveal "many philosophical doctrines."[45] We will recall that Homer has chosen to portray two cities—one at war and one at peace—as the motif for the shield of Achilles.

In addition to the references in Eustathius to attempts to allegorize the two shields, the scholia also preserve an interpretation of Achilles' shield attributed to an Agallis of Corcyra, who apparently was a contemporary of Aristophanes of Byzantium. From their brief remarks it would seem that she regarded the various scenes on the shield as representing the early history of Athens from Erichthonius to the war between Athens and Eleusis and Theseus's journey to Crete. The grounds for the interpretation are the fact that Hephaestus was the father of Erichthonius:

Σ 483: Ἀγαλλὶς ἡ Κερκυραία φησι πιθανῶς ὡς Ἥφαιστος, Ἐριχθονίου πατὴρ ὤν, τὴν ἀρχαιογονίαν τῆς Ἀττικῆς ἐγκατέγραψε τῇ ἀσπίδι. [T]

Agallis of Corcyra says plausibly that Hephaestus, being the father of Erichthonius, portrayed the ancient origins of Attica on the shield.

Whereas Agallis's analysis of the various details on the shield, as preserved in the scholia, does not prove overly convincing and the reason alleged for the allegorization seems questionable, the fact that she did interpret the shield as representing the early history of Athens and the war with Eleusis may well have stimulated Vergil to choose, as his own symbol for Aeneas's shield, the critical moments in the history of Rome which culminate with a description of the battle of Actium (*Aen.* VIII. 626 ff.)

illic res Italas Romanorumque triumphos
haud vatum ignarus venturique inscius aevi
fecerat ignipotens, illic genus omne futurae
stirpis ab Ascanio pugnataque in ordine bella.

The fact that other ancient scholars regarded the two cities on Achilles' shield as representing the city of Troy in war and in peace, and that "Pseudo-Plutarch" saw in the shield an "εἰκών of democracy" serves only to demonstrate the ample precedents that existed for Vergil's choice of subject matter for the shield of Aeneas (*Aen*. VIII. 729–31).[46]

> Talia per clipeum Volcani, dona parentis,
> miratur rerumque ignarus imagine gaudet
> attollens umero famamque et fata nepotum.

One may wonder what the propriety or significance of an early history of Athens might be for Achilles, but the symbolism of Aeneas's shield—the gift of his divine mother—as he raises it on his shoulder, is beyond question.

III

Ancient Views of Homeric Imagery

In recent years classical scholars have been devoting increasing time and energy to the study of image and symbol in Homer and Vergil.[1] On occasion one might view specific observations and appreciations of this "newer criticism" with some scepticism, but for the most part these recreative and often penetrating analyses of the choice and arrangements of the written word have sharpened our sensitivities to a "deeper," or "inner" meaning directly implied or at least latent in the imagery. The question at once arises: how consciously aware was the poet of the "inner" meaning and continuity of his imagery in which we can so often discover a deeper significance which transcends the literal meaning? Perhaps, our symbolic and imagistic approach to ancient poetry is colored in part by our own awareness of contemporary poetic practice and theory, especially inasmuch as scholarly studies of ancient literary theory have revealed remarkably little in the way of critical analysis of this type in Greek and Roman times.[2]

In antiquity Homer was regarded above all as a conscious literary artist, and ancient commentators on the *Iliad* went to great lengths to demonstrate this.[3] It is in their remarks on specific words and phrases, as preserved in the scholia, that a few very concrete examples of ancient views of Homer's technique of imagery appear.[4] No theory as such was formulated, but the specific appreciations of individual passages provide us with a fleeting glimpse of ancient views of imagery. To be sure, it is not the critic who dictates to the mature poet; it is rather the poet who, by his own creativity and originality, provides the new grist for the critic's mill. We may be certain that every conscious literary artist, such as Vergil, would have taken the views of prior criticism into consideration especially on those passages in his archetypes which he might assimilate in his own creative process. Perhaps we possess in the scholia another means by which we can determine Vergil's originality in his adaptation, development, and extension of Homer's imagery, and in addition, a touchstone for our own appreciations of Vergil's use of image and symbol.

The effort to see a deeper, symbolic significance in poetic imagery is closely akin in spirit and means to the attempt of an augur to determine a hidden meaning in portents. Allegorical interpretation of poetry is also quite similar in its quest to discover a veiled intent in the poet's use of words.[5] The first portent in the *Iliad* presents us with a very suitable example as to how the ancient critics extracted a far more extensive symbolic meaning from the occurrence than is implied in the actual interpretation that Homer provides. This particular omen, moreover, has been compared with the Laocoon episode in the *Aeneid*.[6]

In his effort to restrain the Achaeans as they flee towards their ships, Odysseus recalls the portent which had appeared to them some nine years previously at Aulis and how Calchas had interpreted it (*Il.* II. 303 ff.):

> . . . yesterday and before, at Aulis, when the ships of the
> Achaians
> were gathered bringing disaster to the Trojans and Priam,
> and we beside a spring and upon the sacred altars
> were accomplishing complete hecatombs to the immortals
> under a fair plane tree whence ran the shining of water.
> There appeared a great sign; a snake, his back blood-mot-
> tled,
> a thing of horror, cast into the light by the very Olympian,
> wound its way from under the altar and made toward the
> plane tree.
> Thereupon were innocent children, the young of the sparrow,
> cowering underneath the leaves at the uttermost branch tip,

eight of them and the mother was the ninth, who bore these
children.
The snake ate them all after their pitiful screaming,
and the mother, crying aloud for her young ones, fluttered
about him,
and as she shrilled he caught her by the wing and coiled
around her.
After he had eaten the sparrow herself with her children
the god who had shown the snake forth made him a monument,
striking him stone, the son of devious-devising Kronos. . . .

Odysseus then reminds the Achaeans of Calchas's interpretation:
the nine birds represent nine years of warfare; in the tenth,
Troy will fall. That is all.

Scholium Ḻ on this passage, extracted from Porphyry,
preserves the comments of "those who have written on augury
in Homer."[7] In essence, Porphyry tells us that they viewed the
nest high up in the plane tree as representing Troy, "the windy
city"; . . . the wood of the plane tree indicates that the Achaeans
came over the sea in ships to attack Troy; . . . the choice of
sparrows (as opposed to some other bird) was made because the
sparrow is sacred to Aphrodite just as the serpent is sacred to
Athena;[8] . . . the nine sparrows indicate the nine years of
warfare; the tenth year marks the capture and fall of Troy;
. . . the shrieking of the birds represents the wailing of the
captured Trojans; . . . Aristotle regarded the turning of the
snake to stone as an indication of the slowness and difficulty
of the war, while others (who are not named in the scholium)
regarded it as an indication that Troy was left devoid of inhabitants after the Greeks had sacked it and sailed away.[9] At
this point, the scholium becomes somewhat repetitious and may
stem from another source.[10] It resumes:

B 305: . . . τὸ δὲ δένδρον οὖν ἡ ὁδός, ἀλλὰ καὶ ἡ πορεία
τοῦ δράκοντος οὐκ οὖσα ὀρθὴ φύσει οὐδὲ εὐθεῖαν τὴν
ὁδὸν τοῖς Ἕλλησιν ἐσήμαινεν, ὁποία ἐγένετο καὶ αὐτοῖς
ἀπιοῦσί τε καὶ ὑποστρέφουσιν. οὐδὲ τὸ "ἐλελιξάμενος
πτέρυγος λάβεν" (B 316) ἐστὶν ὡς πρὸς μαντείαν ἄχρη-
στον · ἐδήλου δὲ τὸν τρόπον καθ' ὃν τὴν Ἴλιον ἔμελλον
ἐκπορθήσειν οἱ Ἕλληνες. οὐ γὰρ ἐκ τοῦ εὐθέος ἐκράτησαν

καὶ εἶλον, ἀλλ' ἀναχθέντες ἀπὸ τῆς Τρωάδος, εἶθ' ὑπο-
στρέψαντες, ὅ ἐστιν εἰπεῖν "ἐλελιξάμενοι." [B]

The tree, then, is the path [to the city], but [the fact that]
the serpent's mode of travel is not straight by nature indicates that the path of the Greeks was not direct in that
they depart and [then] turn back. Nor is the [phrase] 'he
caught her by the wing and coiled about her' without significance for augury; it showed the manner in which the Greeks
were about to sack Troy, for they did not overcome and
capture it by direct [means, openly], but setting sail from
the Troad, they then turned back, which is to say, 'coiling'.

The point of interest here is that in the eyes of the scholiasts
this one word becomes an image symbolic of the devious means
by which the Greeks sacked Troy.

In the *Iliad* Odysseus tells us that Calchas interpreted the
portent simply as an indication of the length of time it would
take until the Greeks should capture the city. Whether or not
Homer meant to imply all that the scholiasts saw in the portent
is highly questionable, but for the purpose of this study the
query need not come under discussion.[11] The point is, however,
that such close correspondences between Homer's portent and
what in accordance with tradition (if outside the scope of the
Iliad) actually did occur at Troy, was seized upon by the ancient
commentators and exploited in their exegesis of the passage.
One would naturally expect that commentators on augury would
attempt to interpret portents fully and to see in them as much
foreshadowing of the future as possible in each and every
detail. This is an easier matter for the literary critic with the
fait accompli than it is for the actual seer.

A similar examination of parallel points in the portent of
the two serpents that come from Tenedos and destroy Laocoon
and his sons in *Aeneid* II is preserved by Servius (*ad Aen.* II. 203)
and Tiberius Claudius Donatus, though in considerably less
detail. We are told only that the two serpents portend the
imminent danger to Troy which is to come from Tenedos in the
form of the Greek ships under the leadership of the twin chieftains. Bernard W. Knox, however, has taken the remark of the
Latin commentators as a point of departure for his penetrating

analysis of Vergil's use of a "dominant, obsessive metaphor" in *Aeneid* II. In addition to his use of a serpent in his similes, Vergil, as Knox has pointed out, also employs words that are descriptive, primarily, of snakes, such as *insinuare, labi, serpere, volvere,* and so forth, to portray metaphorically the motion of the wooden horse as it creeps into the city, of the fear which seizes the Trojans, of the fire which consumes the city, and of the sleep which embraces them after their celebration at the supposed departure of the Greeks. In short, Knox writes of various images of destruction in this book, "there is one which by its emphatic recurrence comes to dominate all the rest. This is the image of the serpent."[12] Indeed, to the commentators on the portent at Aulis in the *Iliad*, so too did the snake and its coiling seem to possess a deeper meaning as symbolic of the eventual sack of Troy, and especially of the devious means by which the Achaeans contrived to capture it. One image—one word, in fact—becomes representative of the entire *Iliu Persis*. Therefore, in the scholia we are dealing with a discussion of an image whose symbolic meaning Vergil seems clearly to have seized upon and artistically exploited in his own tale of the sack of Troy. Perhaps this is the reason why Vergil chose to emphasize the coils of the snakes when they first appear churning through the sea off Tenedos (*Aen.* II. 203 ff.):

> ecce autem gemini a Tenedo tranquilla per alta
> (horresco referens) immensis orbibus angues
> incumbunt pelago pariterque ad litora tendunt;
> pectora quorum inter fluctus arrecta iubaeque
> sanguineae superant undas; pars cetera pontum
> pone legit sinuatque immensa volumine terga. . . .

The quest for such close correspondence between the descriptive details of Homer's portent and what actually takes place is quite close in method to the scholiasts' observations on similes. The relationship of the simile to the action described (*antapodosis*) is not infrequently seen to correspond in more than one point of the comparison, and in fact, on occasion, will encompass several, including the psychological state or motivation of the figure involved.[13] The similarity of impression upon the reader between metaphor and simile is also discussed in the scholia. In such instances we would seem to be dealing with what has been called in modern times the "continuity of imagery." When Hector saw that Agastrophus had been slain by the Achaeans, he rushed toward the enemy. Aware of his furious onslaught, Diomedes shuddered (ῥίγησε) and said to Odysseus (*Il.* XI. 347 f.):

"Here is this curse, Hector the *huge*, wheeling down upon us
("*νῶϊν δὴ τόδε πῆμα κυλίνδεται, ὄβριμος Ἕκτωρ*")
Let us stand, and hold our ground against him, and beat
him off from us."

Diomedes, however, with a cast of his spear, succeeds in stunning Hector, who then withdraws.

Porphyry, while commenting upon similes some lines earlier, makes the following observation on this particular reference to Hector:

πάλιν δὲ εἰπὼν ἐπὶ τῆς τοῦ Ἕκτορος κατὰ τῶν Ἑλλήνων ὁρμῆς "ὀλοοίτροχος ὡς ἀπὸ πέτρης, ὅν τε κατὰ στεφά-νης ποταμὸς χειμάρροος ὥσει" (*Il.* XIII. 137), κατὰ τὴν αὐτὴν φαντασίαν πεποίηκε περὶ αὐτοῦ λέγοντα τὸν Διομήδην "νῶϊν δὴ τόδε πῆμα κυλίνδεται ὄβριμος Ἕκ-τωρ" (*Il.* XI. 347). ὁ δὲ "ὄβριμος" οἰκεῖος ἀψύχῳ ὁρμῇ. οὐ γὰρ "θρασὺν" ἔφη οὐδὲ "κορυθαίολον", οἷς ἰδίοις αὐτὸν προσαγορεύειν εἴωθεν. [*B* on Λ 269].[14]

Homer has Diomedes use the same imagery concerning Hector when he says, "Here is this curse, Hector the huge [lit., mighty], wheeling down upon us." (*Il.* XI. 347), as he does when he describes Hector's onslaught against the Greeks in *Il.* XIII. 137: ". . . like a great rolling stone from a rock face that a river swollen with winter rain has wrenched from its socket." "Mighty," moreover, is suitable for the onslaught of an inanimate object. He does not say "bold" or "with glancing helmet," words with which he usually distinguishes him ["epithets"].

The term, *phantasia*, occurs frequently in the scholia and appears to mean "creative imagination" or, as here, "the use of imagery." The purpose is defined as to stimulate the "inner vision" and so to create as vivid and as striking an effect as possible upon the reader.[15] The appeal to the "inner eye," or the "mind's eye," is not really much different from what we might term "mental association": the image arouses an additional impression which is then extended to and associated with the object described.[16] The scholiasts felt that Homer, by his choice of the words πῆμα κυλίνδεται ("curse wheels down," *lit.*, ruin is rolling) and ὄβριμος (mighty), was attempting to portray Hector's charge as similar to some wildly irrational force of nature with exactly the same visual impression as he does in the simile some books later when he likens the charge of the Trojan hero to a boulder crashing down a mountain slope destroying all that lies in its path.

The simile which Porphyry refers to occurs when Hector leads an assault on the Greek camp (*Il.* XIII. 136 ff.):

> The Trojans came down on them in a pack, and Hector led them
> raging straight forward, like a great rolling stone from a rock face
> (ἀντικρὺ μεμαώς, ὀλοοίτροχος ὥς ἀπὸ πέτρης)
> that a river swollen with winter rain has wrenched from its socket
> and with immense washing broken the hold of the unwilling rock face;
> the springing boulder flies on, and the forest thunders beneath it;
> and the stone runs unwavering on a strong course, till it reaches
> the flat land, then rolls no longer for all its onrush;
> (ἰσόπεδον, τότε δ᾽ οὔ τι κυλίνδεται ἐσσύμενός περ ·)
> so Hector for a while threatened lightly to break through . . .

until he was met and stopped by a battle line of warriors. The scholia on the word "rolling stone" (ὀλοίτροχος) comment as follows (*Il.* XIII. 137):

λίθος περιφερὴς καὶ στρογγύλος, ὁ ἐν τῷ τρέχειν ὀλοός, ἐπεὶ καταφερόμενος πᾶν τὸ ἐμπῖπτον βλάπτει. [AB] Δημήτριος ὁ γονύπεσος δασύνει, ἵν᾽ ᾖ ὅλος τροχοειδὴς καὶ κατὰ πᾶν μέρος ἀστήρικτος, τῷ δὲ τόνῳ ὡς κακότροπος · οὕτως δὲ καὶ Ἑρμαπίας καὶ Νικίας καὶ Ἀριστέας καὶ Ἀριστόνικος. Κωμανὸς δὲ καὶ Πτολεμαῖος ὁ Ἀσκαλωνίτης ψιλοῦσι καὶ παροξύνουσιν, ἀκούοντες τὸν ἐπὶ τὸ τρέχειν ὀλοὸν καὶ δεινόν. . . . [A]

A round and rolling stone which is destructive in its course since tumbling downwards it harms all that falls in its way. [AB] Demetrius aspirates the word to make it mean altogether round like a wheel and in every way unstable, but in its thrust, malignant; so felt Hermapias, Nicias, Aristaeus, and Aristonicus. Comanus, however, and Ptolemaeus Ascalonites read the *omicron* as unaspirated and [hence] intensify its force, hearing it [as meaning] "destructive" and "terrible" ["dread"]. . . . [A]

Scholium T, here as elsewhere, epitomizes, but retains the essence of the discussion. All three scholia (ABT) conclude with the remark:

καλῶς δὲ βάρβαρον καὶ ἄλογον ὁρμὴν ἀψύχῳ βάρει εἴκασε διὰ παντὸς τόπου κυλινδουμένῳ.

Well did he liken the barbaric and irrational attack to an inanimate mass rolling in every direction.

What the origin of this additional comment was is impossible to say. It is certain, however, that the debate over the precise meaning of the word (ὀλοοίτροχος), from which it arose, began at least as early as the Alexandrian period, long before Porphyry's time.[17]

This appreciation of the simile as representative not merely of the outer, visual aspects of Hector's charge but rather, of his inner, emotional state at the moment is quite in keeping with Porphyry's remarks on Diomedes' imagistic choice of words to call attention to the attack of the Trojan hero in *Iliad* XI. 347. In a sense, then, we are dealing here with a "continuity," or at least a similarity, of imagery which is concerned, according to the scholiasts, with Hector's emotional state. As we shall see, these comments on Hector's "barbaric irrationality" are most similar to contemporary appreciations of Vergil's adaptation of this very same simile to portray Turnus's wild and emotional outburst and attack in *Aeneid* XII. 684 (see pp. 95 ff.).

Such observations as these in the scholia are by no means limited to imagery concerned with boulders. When the Trojans with loud battle cries initially attack the Greek camp in *Iliad*

XIII. 39, like a flame, or stormcloud, the scholiasts approved of the comparison on the grounds that the simile is:

> 39. Φλογὶ ἴσοι. . . . ἠὲ θυέλλῃ) πρὸς τὸ εὐκίνητον ἁρ-
> πακτικὸν ἠχητικόν, ἅμα δὲ καὶ πρὸς τὴν ἄλογον ὁρμήν ·
> ὅθεν οὐδὲ ἐμψύχοις ἀπείκασεν, οἷον λέουσιν ἢ λύκοις · . . . .
> [BT]
>
> Like flame, like a stormcloud) Suitable for their mobility, rapaciousness, and their resounding cries, and at the same time for their irrational onslaught; for this reason they were not likened to animate creatures such as wolves and lions. . . .

Even when Homer likens Hector to animals, similar comments appear in the scholia.[18]

Hector and the Trojans, however, are not the only figures who are likened to lions or "inanimate objects" nor is the wild, irrational aspect of a warrior in the heat of battle the only psychological point of comparison. At the opening of *Iliad* III (23 ff.), as the Greeks and Trojans approach each other for the first time in the epic, Paris steps to the fore and challenges the Argive chieftains to hand to hand combat. Menelaus's reaction is recounted in the following simile:

> Now as soon as Menelaus the warlike caught sight of him making his way with long strides out in front of the army, he was glad, like a lion who comes on a mighty carcass, in his hunger chancing upon the body of a horned stag or wild goat; who eats it eagerly, although against him are hastening the hounds in their speed and the stalwart young men:
> thus Menelaus was happy finding godlike Alexandros. . . .

The scholiasts saw a special significance in the fact that the lion was hungry and that it devoured the carcass even though attacked by a hunting party:

> Γ 24 . . . ὥσπερ οὖν λέοντα παροξύνει λιμὸς καὶ εἰς
> ἀπερίσκεπτον κίνδυνον, οὕτως καὶ νέον ἄνδρα πολεμίου
> ζῆλος εἰς ἀνεκλόγιστον ἀγῶνα προτρέπεται. [ABT]
>
> Just as its hunger spurs the lion on to run into an unforeseen risk, so does a young man's eagerness for war urge him on into an unreasoned struggle [act].

The reference to an unforeseen risk, or danger, in this particular context does not appear pertinent to Menelaus's grim delight and eagerness to confront Paris at long last, but on the other hand, the equation of the lion's hunger to Menelaus's lust for battle is obvious. The comment may simply stem from the efforts, presumably of the Stoics, to extract moral lessons from Homer whenever the possibility presents itself.[19] However, the symbolic meaning that the scholiasts felt was implied in the details of the simile is in keeping with Vergil's use of such details in his similes of predatory beasts (see pp. 78 ff.).[20]

Having seen some of the types of appreciative criticism that the scholiasts bestowed on Homer, let us now turn to a simile which Vergil seems to have adapted from the *Iliad*. When Achilles at last returns to battle in his fury over the death of Patroclus, he storms onto the field; the first to confront him is Aeneas (*Il*. XX. 164 ff.):

> . . . From the other
> side the son of Peleus rose like a lion against him,
> the baleful beast, when men have been straining to kill
> him, the country
> all in the hunt, and he at the first pays them no attention
> but goes his way, only when some one of the impetuous
> young men
> has hit him with the spear he whirls, jaws open, over his
> teeth foam
> breaks out, and in the depth of his chest the powerful
> heart groans;
> he lashes his own ribs with his tail and the flanks on both
> sides
> as he rouses himself with fury for the fight, eyes glaring,
> and hurls himself straight onward on the chance of killing
> some one
> of the men, or else being killed himself in the first onrush.
> So the proud heart and fighting fury stirred on Achilles
> to go forward in the face of great-hearted Aeneas.

The scholiasts, recognizing that the simile has been used to portray the passion of Achilles, point to the wounding of the lion:

Υ 168: δουρὶ βάλῃ) καὶ μὴ τετρωμένον τρωθέντι λέοντι
εἰκάζει · τότε γὰρ ἰσχυρότερος ἑαυτοῦ γίνεται · ἢ ὅτι,
ὅσον τὸ καθ' ἑαυτόν, ἔτρωσεν αὐτὸν ἀκοντίσας ὁ Αἰνείας
(262) · τότε γοῦν ὡς τρωθεὶς ὥρμησεν · τὰ γὰρ πρῶτα
καὶ ἀπέτρεπεν αὐτὸν καθ' "Εκτορος ὡρμημένος. [Τ]

Hit him with the spear) Homer likens him to a wounded
lion though he has not [literally] been wounded; for in that
case, he becomes still more violent; or so that, insofar as
he does so in himself, Aeneas wounded him when he hurled
his spear at him (262); then, at any rate, as though wounded,
he charged; for first of all he tried to dissuade him [from
fighting, see ll. 196–98], having charged out for Hector [see
ll. 76–78].

When Aeneas does hurl his spear, he does not literally wound
Achilles. The wound was taken as a "psychological" one, as
Homer intended, and one which intensifies Achilles' rage still
more since he has been momentarily balked in his fury to
wreak vengeance on Hector.

There is a similar comparison at the very opening of the
last book of the *Aeneid* (XII. 1–9):

Turnus ut infractos adverso Marte Latinos
defecisse videt, sua nunc promissa reposci,
se signari oculis, ultro implacabilis ardet
attollitque animos. Poenorum qualis in arvis
saucius ille gravi venantum vulnere pectus
tum demum movet arma leo, gaudetque comantis
excutiens cervice toros fixumque latronis
impavidus frangit telum et fremit ore cruento:
haud secus accenso gliscit violentia Turno.

Turnus, also, has not literally been assaulted. His pride, however, has suffered a very deep wound, not just by the appearance
of Aeneas as a threat to his proposed marriage to Lavinia, but
even more so by his previous personal defeats in his prosecution
of the war as indicated in the first four lines of the book.[21]

Viktor Pöschl has pointed out that with one exception
Aeneas is never likened to a predatory beast in the whole of
the *Aeneid*, whereas Turnus is frequently compared to such.[22]
The poet, according to Pöschl, has attempted by this means to

portray Turnus as the "personification of demonic forces" in contrast to Aeneas. He continues:

> Moreover, this proves conclusively that Vergil's similes are much more closely connected with the character of the one to whom they apply than are those of Homer. Homer aims to illuminate a particular feature of an event or to represent a sensual impression. Everything else is of secondary importance, which explains why it has been maintained that he is only interested in the *tertium comparationis*. In Vergil's hands the simile is a deeply integrated whole, highlight and focal point for unfolding events. It is a bold and beautiful picture of the idea and destiny of the epic heroes. The poet cannot, therefore, compare Aeneas to a beast of prey.[23]

As we have seen, such similes appeared to the scholiasts to represent far more than a "particular feature of an event or sensual impression." For them Homer's similes clearly corresponded as well to the inner, psychological state or motivation of the figures compared; if the lion, for example, is wounded or hungry, this becomes symbolic of the hero's driving passion or insatiable lust for battle, which could readily urge him on into a dangerous situation and which, presumably, he might well have avoided had he kept a rein on his temper. Moreover, whenever imagery concerning inanimate objects such as fire, wind, storms, or boulders is used, the irrational, indeed barbaric characteristics of the warrior appear to them to have been explicitly emphasized by Homer.[24]

Vergil was working within a literary tradition which he, like any true poet, transcended in creativity and originality of concepts. To appreciate this in as many of its subtle nuances as possible, it is essential that we gain the best available understanding of how the art of Vergil's predecessors was interpreted in his own time. With a fuller understanding of the state of Homeric criticism in antiquity, moreover, we may then be able to determine more accurately what Vergil's purposes were in his adaptation of specific Homeric passages, some of which by his time had taken on widely known symbolic meanings.

Vergil has exploited the imagery as well as its symbolism, using it in familiar contexts as well as in new ones ever varying and extending the meaning in molding it for his own artistic ends. This would help to account for some of the many variations and additions in details of Homeric imagery and their differences in context. It could also well account for the many combinations of several Homeric similes fused into one, and thereby infused with a new and more extended meaning. In this way the illusion of traditional epic would be maintained, while a new and deeper concept of heroism was unfolding.

IV

The Landing at Carthage

The striking similarities between the first book of the Aeneid and the first half of the *Odyssey* have often been noted and discussed.[1] The invocations, the monologues and dialogues of the gods, the storms, the prayers of Odysseus and Aeneas, the safe arrivals in harbor have all been compared and contrasted. The conclusion has been drawn that Vergil, while honoring Homer by imitation, wished at the same time to compete in an *agôn* with his predecessor.[2] It might also be added that with this auspicious beginning of the *Aeneid* Vergil intended specifically and dramatically to contrast the character of Aeneas with that of Odysseus, and that he accomplished this by leading the Roman hero through virtually the same trials and experiences and by fashioning for him almost the same verbal expressions that Homer had given his protagonist.[3]

It is especially interesting to note that the first words spoken by Aeneas (if one excepts the short prayer which he uttered during the storm)[4] serve to illustrate both the difference of character between the two heroes and the thesis that Vergil actually was influenced, or perhaps in this particular case even guided, by the Alexandrian literary criticism of the Homeric poems. The beginning of this first speech by Aeneas to his men is not only based upon one by Odysseus but its circumstance is virtually identical.

In the *Odyssey* Odysseus, in the course of his narrative to the Phaeacians, finishes the tale of his disasterous encounter with the Laestrygonians in which he had lost all but one of his twelve ships. While reconnoitering the island Aeaea, where he and his men had found refuge, he had seen nothing but a wisp of smoke rising in the distance. He was able to kill a stag, and upon his return with it to the shore, he had attempted to raise his men's spirits (*Od.* X. 174–78):

> "Dear friends, sorry as we are, we shall not yet go down into the house of Hades. Not until our day is appointed.
> Come then, while there is something to eat and drink by the fast ship,
> let us think of our food and not be worn out with hunger."

He then urged them to eat what food they had. The next morning he gathered his men together and again addressed them (189–93):

> "Hear my words, my companions, in spite of your hearts' sufferings.
> Dear friends, for we do not know where the darkness is nor the sunrise,
> nor where the sun who shines upon people rises, nor where he sets, then let us hasten our minds and think, whether there is
> any course left open to us. But I think there is none."[5]

Odysseus continues to tell his Phaeacian hosts how his men had completely broken down on recalling their harrowing experiences with the Laestrygonians and the Cyclops.

This situation is quite reminiscent of that of Aeneas and the Trojans after the storm with which the action of the *Aeneid* begins.[6] Aeneas's speech in this circumstance, as Macrobius pointed out, is based largely upon another by Odysseus, though in quite a different situation from that of the *Aeneid*.[7] The occasion of the speech cited by Macrobius is as follows: upon hearing the roar of the waters seething about Scylla's cliffs, the crew became terrified and ceased rowing. Odysseus at once responded in characteristic fashion (*Od.* XII. 208–12):

> "Dear friends, surely we are not unlearned in evils.
> This is no greater evil now than it was when the Cyclops had us cooped in his hollow cave by force and violence,
> but even there, by my courage and counsel and my intelligence,

we escaped away. I think that all this will be remembered
some day too."

Odysseus then suggests to his hosts that he had deliberately
avoided all mention of Scylla lest his men in panic seek refuge
in the hold. Such encouragement as this, together with the
careful avoidance of any reference to yet another fabulous and
savage beast was, as Odysseus points out, altogether necessary
for their safety.

Vergil's *poiêsis* of the landing of the Trojans on the shores
of Africa, while remarkable for its similarity to the comparable
scenes in the *Odyssey*, is even more remarkable for its differences. After Aeneas and the remnant of his ill-fated fleet
had survived the violent storm, the latest of several terrifying
experiences, and had safely landed, he left the ships in search
of some trace of his lost companions, and likewise procured
game for his men. On return to the shore, Aeneas, too, attempted to console his crews (*Aen.* I. 197–209):

> . . . et dictis maerentia pectora mulcet:
> "O socii (neque enim ignari sumus ante malorum),
> o passi graviora, dabit deus his quoque finem.
> vos et Scyllaeam rabiem penitusque sonantis
> accestis scopulos, vos et Cyclopia saxa
> experti; revocate animos maestumque timorem
> mittite; forsan et haec olim meminisse iuvabit.
> per varios casus, per tot discrimina rerum
> tendimus in Latium, sedes ubi fata quietas
> ostendunt; illic fas regna resurgere Troiae.
> durate, et vosmet rebus servate secundis."
>   Talia voce refert curisque ingentibus aeger
> spem vultu simulat, premit altum corde dolorem.

Macrobius's comparison of this pair of speeches is quite
interesting, and his remarks are well taken, even if by now they
do not seem strikingly perceptive (*Sat.* V. 11, 5):

> in his quoque versibus Maro extitit locupletior interpres
> (*Aen.* I. 198 ff. et *Od.* XII. 208–12). Ulixes ad socios unam
> commemoravit aerumnam: hic ad sperandam praesentis mali
> absolutionem gemini casus hortatur eventu. deinde ille
> obscurius dixit

καί που τῶνδε μνήσεσθαι ὀΐω [I. 212]
hic apertius
    forsan et haec olim meminisse iuvabit.
sed et hoc, quod vester [Maro] adiecit, solacii fortioris est.
suos enim non tantum exemplo evadendi sed et spe futurae felicitatis animavit, per hos labores non solum sedes
quietas sed et regna promittens.[8]

Several other noteworthy differences in these two speeches
have been pointed out by various modern scholars. R. S.
Conway observed one of these differences:

> . . . for Odysseus' boast (XII. 206 ff.) of his valor,
> counsel, and foresight in previous trials, Aeneas
> substitutes a reverent faith in divine protection
> (199, 205) and confidence in his men's courage (202):
> the hesitation of *forsan* reflects Homer's που, etc.[9]

Odysseus had already been told that he would receive no aid
from the gods, whereas Aeneas is continually aided by them,
and it is indeed by reference to divine aid that he endeavors
to console his companions. As V. Pöschl points out, Aeneas's
words reveal his *pietas* and *magnitudo animi*:[10]

> Homer portrays a courageous man in a most hazardous
> situation . . . who gives clever and discreet commands.
> Vergil, on the other hand, portrays Aeneas as a magnani-
> mous spirit who presses on towards a magnificent goal.

To revert, however, to the opening words of Aeneas's exhortation, "*o passi graviora . . .*"; it is surprising that these words
have been compared to "Bear up, my heart. You have had
worse to endure before this/on that day when. . . ." (*Od.* XX.
17), words which Odysseus uttered to himself while pondering
the evil done by the suitors.[11] If Vergil did indeed derive these
words from any one Homeric passage, rather than to develop,
"This is no greater evil now than it was. . . ." (*Od.* XII. 209),
it must surely have been the words with which Odysseus addressed his men after his reconnaissance of Aeaea, "in spite of
your hearts' sufferings" (κακά περ πάσχοντες ἑταῖροι, *Od.* X.
189).[12] Vergil might merely have raised the substantive to the
comparative degree, thereby securing a more poignant effect.
Thus, not only would Vergil appear to have appropriated the

situation from *Odyssey* X, he may also have adapted the first line of Odysseus's address given on that very occasion.

In this same episode, Odysseus's first speech after the Greeks had found safe anchorage, while purporting to be an encouraging word to the crew, did little more than urge them to eat and to remind them that the "fateful day" had not yet come upon them. A scholiast, however, did make the observation that that night Odysseus had withheld the results of his expedition from his crew, doubtless with tacit approval:

κ 185: ἦμος δ᾽ ἠέλιος κατέδυ) οὐδὲ μετὰ τὴν τροφὴν λέγει πρὸς αὐτοὺς περὶ τῆς κατασκοπῆς, ἀλλ᾽ ἐᾷ τὴν πρώτην. [HQ][13]

But when the sun went down) He does not speak to them about the expedition after eating, but lets [it go] for the present.

Odysseus's speech of the following morning, however, was criticized by the scholiasts, among them in all probability, Aristarchus himself:

κ 189: ὦ φίλοι, οὐ γὰρ τ᾽ ἴδμεν ὅπη ζόφος) ταῦτα δὲ λέγει οὐκ ἀπορῶν, ἀλλὰ δεινοπαθῶν τοῖς παροῦσιν. Ἄλλως. ἄλογόν ἐστι τὸ τοὺς ἑταίρους ἀθυμίᾳ περιβάλλειν. λύεται δὲ ἐκ τοῦ καιροῦ. πρὸς γὰρ τὸ δεῖν σκέψασθαι τοὺς οἰκήτορας τῶν τόπων ἥρμοττε τὴν ἀπορίαν τῶν χωρίων εἰπεῖν. [QT]
κ 193: ἐγὼ δ᾽ οὐκ οἴομαι) τοῦτο εἶναι διὰ μέσου φησὶν Ἀρίσταρχος ὡς ἂν ἀπαλγήσαντος τοῦ Ὀδυσσέως ἰδίᾳ ἀναπεφωνῆσθαι. [HQ][14]

"Dear friends, for we do not know where the darkness is") He says this not because he is at a loss, but complaining bitterly over their present circumstance. In another sense: it is unreasonable for him to cast his companions into despondency. [The question] is solved by the circumstance; for to speak of their ignorance [lit., difficult straits] of the place well suits their need to spy on the inhabitants of the area.

"But I think there is none.") Aristarchus says that this is in parenthesis on the grounds that if Odysseus were despondent, [these words] would have been uttered to himself [lit., privately].

One certainly does wonder, despite the solutions of the *lutikoi*, why Odysseus appears to have discouraged his men whose morale he had ostensibly, at least, if not effectively, attempted to raise the night before.[15] There is an obvious need to send out a scouting party, but this is somewhat obscured by Odysseus's pessimistic conclusion to his address. One might thus agree with Aristarchus(?) that the final phrase, "But I think there is none," ought to be placed in parenthesis on the grounds that Odysseus would have been better represented as having uttered it to himself. We must not, however, lose sight of the fact that this speech is but part of Odysseus's narrative to the Phaeacians.

It will be helpful to examine once more Vergil's handling of the thought of which Pöschl writes that the impression of Aeneas's inner greatness is still more intensified by having the hero's words move from the depths of enormous pain and sorrow:

> talia voce refert curisque ingentibus aeger
> spem vultu simulat, premit altum corde dolorem.[16]

It is precisely this suppression of his own despair and anxiety in the face of his companions' utter despondency that contrasts Aeneas so sharply with Odysseus. The situation and most of the words are Homeric, but the composition of the whole is purely and typically Vergilian.

It is true, of course, that Odysseus's men were fated to be lost, not simply "by the gods," but by the exigencies of the plot itself, which required that the hero arrive home in Ithaca, alone and unrecognized.[17] Vergil, on the other hand, was composing an epic of the founding of what had already become the mightiest nation and empire on earth, so it was imperative that Aeneas have the utmost concern for the physical as well as the spiritual well-being of all his men. That Aeneas, at the opening of the *Aeneid*, should privately harbor grave doubts about the success of his as yet not fully realized mission at such a crisis is not merely natural, it is in itself a most critical facet of Vergil's characterization of his own hero.[18]

In short Vergil seems to have appropriated Odysseus's landing at Aeaea as follows: for the words of Odysseus on this occasion, he has substituted, within the framework of the original, part of another speech from the *Odyssey* and fused the whole together for his own artistic purpose. At the same time, it would also seem that Vergil rejected Odysseus's sentiment, and by his acceptance of the Alexandrian exegesis, compelled the reader to compare the Homeric passage with Aeneas and his action. This contrast of character between Odysseus and Aeneas is too carefully contrived to be fortuitous and it is quite unlikely that Vergil was unaware of the traditional commentaries and their criticism of this passage in the *Odyssey*.[19]

This deliberate contrast of characterization is again conspicuous in the immediately ensuing action. The next morning Aeneas carefully concealed his ships and set out to explore the area. On the way he was met by Venus, disguised as a huntress in search of her sisters.[20] This encounter has been likened to several in the *Odyssey*.

Odysseus's first words to Nausicaa are remarkable for their subtlety, as Homer points out (*Od.* VI. 148–52):

> So blandishingly and full of craft he began to address her:
> "I am at your knees, O queen. But are you mortal or
> goddess?
> If indeed you are one of the gods who hold wide heaven,
> then I must find in you the nearest likeness to Artemis
> the daughter of great Zeus, for beauty, figure, and stature...."

Odysseus continues to flatter her with a most courtly address while telling her of his misfortunes.

The scholiasts on this passage discussed at considerable length Odysseus's flattery of Nausicaa, especially his address to her as a divinity:

> ζ 149: γουνοῦμαί σε, ἄνασσα) ... καὶ τὸ μὲν ἄντικρυς
> ὡς θεῷ διαλέγεσθαι κολακείας ὑποψίαν ἐμποιήσειν ἔμελ-
> λεν, ἐπιδιστάζων δὲ ἀξιοπιστότερον τὸν λόγον καθίστη-
> σιν, ὡς ἂν καθελκόμενος ὑπὸ τῆς δόξης. καλῶς δὲ καὶ
> τῇ τάξει · ἐπὶ πρώτην γὰρ ἧκε τὴν τῆς θεότητος ὑπόνοιαν,
> ὡς ἐπὶ τοῦτο μᾶλλον ῥέπων. [HQ][21]

"I am at your knees, O queen.") An outright address to
her as a goddess would have created the impression of
flattery, but as if in doubt, he presents a more trustworthy
approach, as though he were drawn over to this opinion by
her outward appearance. Nicely arranged; for he has uttered
his suspicion of her divinity at the beginning [of his address],
as if rather inclining toward it.

The whole speech is indeed a clever device, quite worthy of
the wily Odysseus, and not at all unlike another which he,
while in disguise, delivers to Athena in a later book.[22] It was
at least questionable to the ancient scholars whether Odysseus
did in fact believe that Nausicaa was a divinity.

Aeneas's response is entirely different. It is, first of all,
direct and devoid of all subtlety (*Aen*. I. 326–30):

"nulla tuarum audita mihi neque visa sororum,
o quam te memorem, virgo? namque haud tibi vultus
mortalis, nec vox hominem sonat; o, dea certe
(an Phoebi soror? an Nympharum sanguinis una?),
sis felix nostrumque leves, quaecumque, laborem. . . ."

Aeneas continues to inform her of their disasterous voyage and
then asks for directions, promising a sacrifice in her honor.
Venus replies by denying any connection with the gods but
answers his questions, telling him the history of Dido. In
response to her inquiry as to his own identity, Aeneas replies,
"O dea. . . ." and (375–79):

"nos Troia antiqua, si vestras forte per auris
Troiae nomen iit, diversa per aequora vectos
forte sua Libycis tempestas appulit oris.
sum pius Aeneas, raptos qui ex hoste Penatis
classe veho mecum, fama super aethera notus. . . ."

As has been pointed out, Aeneas still believes that he is speaking
to a divinity of some sort, despite Venus's disclaimer, and the
epithet which he applies to himself must be considered in this
light.[23]

These two lines (378–79) with which Aeneas reveals his
identity are surely meant to be compared with the equally
celebrated lines with which Odysseus finally makes himself
known to the Phaeacians (*Od*. IX. 19–20):

"I am Odysseus son of Laertes, known before all men
for the study of crafty designs, and my fame goes up to
the heavens."[24]

The scholiasts comment again at some length on these lines,
emphasizing that Odysseus so phrases his words as to improve
his chances of gaining his due honor from the Phaeacians:

ι 20: μεν κλέος οὐρανὸν ἵκει) διὰ δόλους ἔνδοξός εἰμι.
ὁ γὰρ δόλος καὶ ἐπὶ ἀγαθοῦ τάσσεται · νῦν δὲ ἐπὶ ἐγκω-
μίου τοῦτο λέγει. ὑπερβολὴ γὰρ δόξης τὸ μέχρι θεῶν
ἐφθακέναι τὸ κλέος. ταῦτα δὲ πρὸς σύστασιν ἑαυτοῦ λέγει,
ἵνα κατ᾽ ἀξίαν τιμηθῇ ὑπὸ τῶν Φαιάκων. ἤδη γὰρ καὶ
προμεμαρτύρηται ὑπὸ τοῦ κιθαρῳδοῦ. [BQ][25]

". . . my fame goes up to the heavens.") I am held in es-
teem because of my "crafty designs." [He says this] because his cunning is devised for the good; and now he says
this as praise [for himself]. His phrase that his fame has
attained to the gods is an excessive statement of his repute,
but he says it as his introduction of himself so that the
Phaeacians will honor him in accordance with his worth;
for indeed he had already previously been sung of by the
bard.

It should, however, be remembered that it was Odysseus himself who had first requested Demodocus to sing the tale of the
Trojan Horse.

Vergil would accordingly appear to have carefully de-
signed the opening scenes of the *Aeneid* to declare unequiv-
ocally that his would not be a hero whose fame and reputation rested on his wiles: Aeneas is known by his *pietas*. This
contrast of Homeric and Vergilian characterization is revealed
straightway by the very first words of Aeneas in the prayer
which he utters during the storm that opens the *Aeneid*. The
character of the two heroes is again sharply contrasted by the
speeches each delivers to his men after they have landed on
an unknown and deserted shore, and culminates with the famed
lines with which each reveals his identity. Odysseus subtly
addresses the maiden in the hopes that his flattery will gain
his ends (so the ancient commentators understood his hesitation).
Aeneas, on the other hand, in the throes of a great despair,

torn by anxiety and wearied as a result of his terrifying experiences, cries out bitterly to the maiden, who, he is certain
("*o dea, certe* . . ."), is a goddess. In a different situation, but
also to impress his audience, Odysseus cleverly and dramatically cites his reputation as a warrior who lives by his wiles,
and again his purpose is to gain honor for himself. Aeneas,
on the contrary, points to his *pietas* in his quest for the land
promised him by the gods.

One may safely conclude that had Vergil not wished to
make such a comparison of character at the very outset of his
epic, he would not have made such meticulous and elaborate
use of Homeric materials in leading his hero "in the wake of
Odysseus." Vergil knew his Homer well, and from his characterization of Aeneas it would also seem that he was aware
of the traditional criticism and exegesis on the passages he
drew so carefully from the *Odyssey*.

V

Nisus and Euryalus

Although the *Dolonia* of *Iliad* X and the nocturnal adventure
of Nisus and Euryalus in *Aeneid* IX might appear to the casual
reader to be fertile ground for comparative analysis, the differences between these two episodes have actually been judged
to be so great as to preclude saying anything more specific
than that Vergil "derived inspiration" from the Homeric tale.[1]
Before accepting this view, however, we should carefully consider not only the validity of this assertion, but also why, in
view of so many undeniable similarities, is it so. Is it possible
that some of the many variations from the *Dolonia* in *Aeneid*
IX derived from the ancient interpretations and criticisms
levelled against the original—criticisms and appreciations such
as those now preserved in the Homeric scholia?

Nyktegoria

When the *Dolonia* begins, it is already night and the Greek
encampment is bedded down. Agamemnon, however, is rest-
lessly awake, tormented by the plight of his forces (*Il.* X. 11–13):

> Now he would gaze across the plain to the Trojan camp
> wondering
> at the number of their fires that were burning in front of
> Ilion,
> toward the high calls of their flutes and pipes, the murmur
> of people.

The scholia on these lines reveal that the ancient scholars
wondered how Agamemnon could "see" so much from his camp,

which lies behind the Achaean wall. They proceed, then, to provide explanations which are typical of their approach:

K 11: ὅτ' ἐς πεδίον τὸ Τρωικὸν ἀθρήσειεν) ἢ ὅτι ἐφ' ὕψους ἡ βασιλικὴ σκηνή, ἢ ὅτι οἱ Τρῶες "ἐπὶ θρωσμῷ πεδίοιο" (160). ἔνιοι τὸ "ἀθρήσειεν" ἐπὶ τοῦ νοῦ ἀκούουσιν. . . . [BT]²

K 12 : θαύμαζεν πυρά) πῶς, φησὶν, Ἀγαμέμνων ἐντὸς τοῦ τείχους ὑπάρχων ἐθαύμαζε τὰ πυρά, τὴν ἀρχὴν μηδὲ βλέπων αὐτὰ διὰ τοῦ τείχους; καὶ ῥητέον ὅτι βασιλεὺς ὑψηλοτάτην εἶχε σκηνὴν ἵν' εὐχερῶς θεωρεῖν πάντα δύνηται. [A]

Now he would gaze across the plain to the Trojan camp) Either because the king's camp was on a height, or because the Trojans were "on ground rising from the plain." (160) Some take "gaze" to mean "in the mind. . . ."
Wondered at the fires) How, he says, does Agamemnon, actually inside the wall, wonder at the fires, since he could not look at them at all through the wall? But it must be said that the king had the highest camp in order to be able to observe everything readily.

Trifling as this criticism is, it is there for all to read and it would not have escaped Vergil's scholarly eye, for he states pointedly at the very beginning of his own *Nyktegoria* that the Trojan camp is on high ground and that the activity of the Rutulians can be seen as they settle down for the night.³ Nisus, the *portae custos*, is pictured as looking out over the enemy camp when there forms in his mind the plan of volunteering to carry the news of the day's battle to the absent Aeneas (IX. 168).

Agamemnon resolves to arouse Nestor and seek his advice; the two men then summon together the other chieftains of the Greek hosts. The exact location of this assembly has been puzzling to both ancient and modern commentators. Nestor, followed closely by the chosen Achaean heroes, stepped across the moat (*Il.* X. 198–201):

After they had crossed the deep-dug ditch they settled
on clean ground, where there showed a space not cumbered
with corpses

of the fallen, a place whence Hector the huge had turned
back
from destroying the Argives, after the night had darkened
about him.

The scholiasts, from Aristotle on, raised the question why the
assembly was held beyond the safety of the walls. The answers
which have survived are that Nestor wished to avoid a general
disturbance in the camp, especially since the Greeks were already
in deep distress over the results of the day's battle. It would
be unfitting, the scholia continue, if in an attempt to send out
spies, the leaders themselves should hesitate to pass beyond the
safety of the wall; by so doing, their daring would serve to
encourage the scouts.[4] At any rate, Vergil avoided the "problem"
entirely.

After Nisus, of his own accord, had conceived the plan to
carry the news of the day's battle to Aeneas, he immediately
went to his superiors, already in counsel (*Aen.* IX. 226–30):

> ductores Teucrum primi, delecta iuventus,
> consilium summis regni de rebus habebant,
> quid facerent quisve Aeneae iam nuntius esset.
> stant longis adnixi hastis et scuta tenentes
> castrorum et campi medio. . . .

Modern scholars have noted that Vergil has greatly compressed
the events leading up to the meeting.[5] The location of the
assembly is the center of the Trojan camp, and so, inasmuch
as they are besieged, they are within the safety of the walls.
Avoiding the curious situation in the *Dolonia*, Vergil may well
have substituted the historical Roman *praetorium*. If this is so
(there have been objections)[6] we have another instance of an
attempt by Vergil to establish a legendary precedent for the
well-known Roman military "command headquarters."

In the Homeric tale the Greek heroes, reaching the site
chosen for the assembly, sit down (202). In the *Aeneid*, as if
in deliberate contrast, Vergil has portrayed the Trojan leaders
as standing, leaning on their spears, their hands on their shields.
This, too, according to Servius, is a Roman custom (*ad Aen.*
IX. 227):

adnixi hastis: mira facies consilii; in rebus dubiis non sedent
sed stant. *adnixi hastis* ostendit iam eos diurna statione
fatigatos. quod autem stant et Romani moris est et bellicae
necessitatis. . . .

Hector, too, when he addresses the Trojans outside the Greek
camp (*Il.* VIII. 489 ff.) is likewise portrayed as leaning on his
spear. The scholiasts commented to the effect that Aristarchus
regarded the lines as more suitable, here, than in book VI where
they first appear, because Hector is now haranguing the army.[7]
A second scholium continues:

Θ 494: ἔγχος ἔχε) ὡς ἐν πολέμῳ δημηγορῶν ἀντὶ σκήπρου
τῷ δόρατι χρῆται, τὰ σημεῖα τῆς ἀνδρ<ε>ίας προβαλ-
λόμενος. [BT]

Held the spear) He uses a spear instead of the scepter since
he is addressing the assembly in war, putting forth the
tokens of valor.

It could be that Vergil wished to imply the same.

These points of departure from the opening lines of the
Dolonia may indeed seem trivial and insignificant, but they are
highly characteristic of Vergil's meticulous approach to composition and his methods of appropriating Homeric materials.
Sensitive to the grounds of the criticism, if not to the criticism
itself, Vergil has given the scene a Roman flavor, "improving"
upon the original version in such a way as to invite comparison.[8]

Turning now to the treatment of the assembly, let us first
consider two statements from standard works which call attention to one major difference between the two episodes:

The hint of the episode of Nisus and Euryalus is from Homer's
Dolonia; but the effect produced is due entirely to the art
of the younger poet. In the Homeric story we sympathize
neither with Dolon nor his captors: the former fails where
he did not deserve to succeed: the success of the latter is
too complete to call for much enthusiasm.[9]

The poet [Vergil] loses no opportunity to bring out the
pathos of his story and the impulses that determine the
outer action.[10]

Both remarks are true to a degree. But in what respects has
Vergil modified the structural details of the outer as well as
inner action?

Nisus is well aware of the danger which confronts him—
so much so that he tries, initially, to dissuade his friend from
accompanying him, fearing for his friend's safety (IX. 207 ff.).
This is in sharp contrast with the *Dolonia*, where Diomedes'
willingness to volunteer is conditioned by his wish to be allowed to have a companion (*Il.* X. 222 ff.). Such a consideration,
however, as fear for one's friend in the danger of such a mission,
key to the pathos of the Vergilian episode, does not figure in
the *Dolonia*, except for one possible reference. Agamemnon
speaks his only words during the assembly in an effort to prevent
his brother from being chosen to accompany Diomedes (233–39).
The scholium on the next line, "So he spoke, and was frightened
for Menelaos of the fair hair," indicates that these words were
omitted by Zenodotus and athetized by Aristarchus on the
grounds that they are superfluous and do not add anything to
the thought already expressed in the preceding lines.[11] It is
also worth noting what the scholium says of the word ἕταρον,
used by Agamemnon (235):

> K 242: εἰ μὲν δὴ ἕταρόν γε κελεύετε) ὅτι ἕταρον νῦν οὐ
> φίλον, ἀλλὰ συνεργὸν λέγει. ἡ δὲ ἀναφορὰ πρὸς τὸ ἑτα-
> ρίσσαιτο [*Il.* XIII. 456] ἀντὶ τοῦ συνεργὸν λάβοι. [A][12]
>
> "If indeed you tell me to pick out my companion.") [Note?]
> that he now says companion, not friend, but accomplice.
> A repetition occurs in XIII, 456, "find some Trojan to be
> his companion" in place of choosing an accomplice.

It would seem likely from these remarks that some question
had been raised as to why the term "friend" was not used—a
point not raised by Homer. Herein lies a most important crux
in the development of the plot of the Vergilian episode and
the most obvious point of difference between the two versions
of the expedition.

While discussing the plan to send out spies, Nestor seems
to depreciate the risk involved, or so it seemed to the ancient
commentators. Nestor's speech follows (X. 204–13):

> "O my friends, is there no man who, trusting in the daring
> of his own heart, would go among the high-hearted Trojans?
> So he might catch some enemy, who straggled behind them,

or he might overhear some thing that the Trojans are saying,
what they deliberate among themselves, and whether they
purpose
to stay where they are, close to the ships, or else to with-
draw back
into their city, now that they have beaten the Achaeans.
Could a man learn this, and then come back again to us
unhurt, why huge and heaven-high would rise up his glory
among all people, and an excellent gift would befall him. . . ."

The scholia comment:

K 206: ἔλοι ἐσχατόωντα) ζωγρῆσαι πρὸς τὸ πυθέσθαι
τὰ παρὰ τοῖς πολεμίοις. διὰ δὲ τοῦ "ἐσχατόωντα" τὸ
ἀκίνδυνον ὑπέφηνε τῆς πράξεως καὶ ἀντιπαρέβαλε τῷ
"μέγα κέν οἱ ὑπουράνιον κλέος εἴη" (212). [BT]
K 212: ἀσκηθής) πανταχόθεν προτρέπεται, τῷ εὐχερεῖ,
τῷ ἀκινδύνῳ, τῷ εὐκλεεῖ. [BT]

Catch some straggler) [i.e.,] to capture him alive to learn
the enemy's plans. By his use of the word "straggler" he
intimates that the deed is without risk and contrasts this
with "why huge and heaven-high would rise up his glory."
Unhurt, why huge and heaven-high) He urges them on in
every way, the ease [of the mission], the lack of risk, the
glorious reputation.

Although it is true that the scholiasts are doubtless merely commenting on the subtleties of Nestor's appeal, the fact remains
that there is no real stress at the outset, or for that matter,
in the entire book, on the risks involved in such a venture. As
the scholiast points out, Nestor contrasts the great fame to be
won with the ease of the mission.

Hector, on the other hand, in the Trojan assembly during
the same night and presumably at the same time, first asks for
a volunteer, then describes the reward for the venture, and only
then what it is he wants accomplished (X. 308 ff.):

"to go close to the swift-running ships and find out for us
whether the swift ships are guarded, as they were before this,
or whether now the Achaians who are beaten under our hands
are planning flight among themselves, and no longer are
willing
to guard them by night, now that stark weariness has broken
them."

Hector is indeed asking quite a bit of his volunteer.[13]

In this respect, then, Vergil has chosen to alter fundamentally the spirit of this episode in his version. By emphasizing the danger (IX. 207 ff.), he has developed the conversation between the two friends in such a way as to enlist our sympathy and concern for them.

At the opening of his speech, as we have read, Nestor asked for a volunteer; the scholiasts expressed their admiration for the way in which this was done:

Κ 204: οὐκ ἂν δή τις) ἐξ αὐτοῦ τοῦ πράγματος ἄρχεται· οὐκ ἔδει γὰρ προοιμίων, ἀλλ' ὀξυβουλίας ἐν τῷ τοιούτῳ καιρῷ. ὑποθετικῶς δὲ ἄρχεται, οὐ προστακτικῶς. εὖ δὲ καὶ τὸ μὴ ἕνα ἐκλέξασθαι· ἐλύπησε γὰρ <ἂν> αὐτὸν ὡς καταφρονῶν τῆς αὐτοῦ σωτηρίας, καὶ τοὺς λοιποὺς ᾔσχυνεν. φιλοτιμίαν οὖν τοῖς ἀρίστοις εἰς ἀλλήλους ἐμβαλὼν τοὺς ἀτόλμους οὐκ ἤλεγξεν, ἀλλ' ἡσυχίαν αὐτοῖς ἀνεπίφθονον δέδωκεν. εὖ δὲ καὶ τὸ αὐθαίρετον· οὐ γὰρ "ἐμοί," φησί, "πεπίθοιτο," ἀλλ' "ἑῷ αὐτοῦ θυμῷ" καὶ "τολμήεντι," ὅ ἐστι περιεκτικὸν τῆς προκειμένης πράξεως. [BT]

"Is there no man?") He begins with the task itself; for there is no need for an introduction, but rather for quickness of counsel at such a critical moment. He begins with a suggestion, not a command. The fact that he did not choose a particular individual is good, for he would have [in that case] offended him as dealing contemptuously with his safety and put the rest to shame. Therefore, by sowing the seeds of ambitious rivalry among the best, he did not treat the cowardly with contempt but rather gave them a graceful escape. The fact that he makes the choice voluntary is also good, for he does not say "Let him trust in me" but rather "in the daring of his own heart," which is the all-embracing [requisite] for the task at hand.

At the similar council in the Trojan camp, Hector begins his speech (X. 303 f.):

"Who would take upon him this work and bring it to fulfilment
for a huge price? The reward will be one that will suffice him."

He continues, offering a chariot and two horses—the best of the Greek host; fame will also be his as a result of the undertaking.[14]

The scholiasts comment at this point on the manner in which the two chieftains make their requests, and upon the fact that Nestor offers a "gift" which is in his power to bestow, while Hector "ignominiously" offers "payment" which he does not have:

K 303: τίς κέν μοι τόδε ἔργον) ὁ μὲν Ἕκτωρ μετὰ προστά-
ξεως τὸν ὑπακουσόμενον τῇ χρείᾳ καλεῖ, ὁ δὲ Νέστωρ
ὑποτίθεται. καὶ οἱ μὲν ἃ ἔχουσιν ἐπαγγέλονται, ὁ δὲ ἃ
οὐκ ἔχει, καὶ οἱ μὲν δῶρον, ὁ δὲ ἀτίμως μισθόν. [BT]
καὶ πρῶτον ἔταξε τὸν μισθόν· διὸ δελεάζεται ὁ υἱὸς
τοῦ πολυχρύσου. (315) [T][15]

"Who would take upon him this work?") Hector calls upon someone to heed his request with a command, but Nestor makes a proposal.   They [the Greeks] announce as a gift what they have, while he ignominiously offers as payment what he does not have. [BT] At the very beginning he prescribed the pay; therefore the son of the rich man is caught by the bait. [T]

Vergil, on the other hand, quite in contrast to both speeches of the *Iliad*, and in keeping with the spirit of the scholiasts' observations, has made Nisus's motivation to undertake the venture truly spontaneous and the decision, truly voluntary. In this way he has emphasized, at least initially, the heroism and chivalry of the offer. As Nisus stands musing at his post, he suddenly says to Euryalus, called *comes* (IX. 184–87):

"... dine hunc ardorem mentibus addunt,
Euryale, an sua cuique deus fit dira cupido?
aut pugnam, aut aliquid iamdudum invadere magnum
mens agitat mihi, nec placida contenta quiete est."

The sentiment, *mens agitat mihi*, is exactly that which Nestor expresses, but in the *Aeneid*, it springs from the heart, that is, it is truly αὐθαίρετον, as expressed in the scholia (BT on K 204). Nisus, to be sure, knows that Aeneas must be summoned (cf. l. 192), but he does not need the express request of a superior officer to motivate him to spring to the need of his people. He

unfolds his plan to Euryalus, and then speaks of the reward he
seeks (194–96):

> "si tibi quae posco promittunt (nam mihi facti
> fama sat est), tumulo videor reperire sub illo
> posse viam ad muros ad moenia Pallantea."[16]

Since Nisus has volunteered his services, there can have been
no prior mention of rewards or gifts. After Aletes learns of the
gesture, however, he responds (247–54):

> "Di patrii, quorum semper sub numine Troia est,
> non tamen omnino Teucros delere paratis,
> cum talis animos iuvenum et tam certa tulistis
> pectora."—sic memorans umeros dextrasque tenebat
> amborum et vultum lacrimis atque ora rigabat.—
> "quae vobis, quae digna, viri, pro laudibus istis
> praemia posse rear solvi? pulcherrima primum
> di moresque dabunt vestri. . . ."

Accordingly, Vergil has created a warrior who truly volunteers
of his own accord to undertake a dangerous mission quite in
contrast with Nestor's proposal (cf. scholia on K 204 and 303)
and offer of a gift, even as the scholiasts had contrasted this
with Hector's methods of asking for a volunteer and "crass"
reference to payment.[17]

For Vergil, true virtue will be its own reward. Aletes adds,
however, that Aeneas and Ascanius will undoubtedly present
them with fitting rewards. Ascanius at once swears to this and
promises Nisus several gifts. In much the same extravagant
way that Hector promises to give Dolon Achilles' horses and
chariot, he includes the horses and chariot of Turnus. All this,
however, is after the pair have offered their services, and in
another departure from the unqualified terms of Hector's promises, Ascanius prefaces a condition (267–68):

> "si vero capere Italiam sceptrisque potiri
> contigerit victori et praedae dicere sortem. . . ."

In comparison with the scholiasts' remarks on Hector's
stipulation of payment for the exploit (K 303), the Latin scholiast's comment on Ascanius's speech is most instructive of
Vergil's method of appropriation (*ad Aen.* IX. 267):

vidisti quo Turnus equo: melior oeconomia: Nisum noluit
inducere postulantem equum Turni praemii loco, sed hones-
tius facit ultro offerri, cum Homerus fecerit Dolonem Achillis
currus improbe postulantem.

We are thus once more invited, as it were, to recall the desires
and demands of Dolon and the contrast between the motives
and the character of the Homeric and Vergilian figures in all
that precedes the actual adventures of the spies.

Before leaving the matter of rewards for successful exploits,
let us note that: (1) when Nisus thinks of making the sally
alone, he speaks of a reward, not for himself, but for Euryalus.
He suspects that he might not return, and if killed, he wishes
to provide for his younger friend. For himself, the glory of the
deed alone, will suffice. (2) When it is settled that both will
go, Nisus never speaks of a reward of any kind. (3) Euryalus,
on the other hand, thinks only of the welfare of his mother,
who, if they fail, will be left alone and resourceless. He says
to Ascanius (290–92):

"at tu, oro, solare inopem et succurre relictae.
hanc sine me spem ferre tui, audentior ibo
in casus omnis."

This seems to indicate that he, too, has grave fears that they
might not succeed. The contrast between the mood here and
in the *Dolonia* (apart from its function in the *Iliad*) is striking.
In the *Dolonia*, everything is quite positive: the risks are
minimized, if only for the purpose of encouraging volunteers,
awards are offered or demanded, and the success of the venture
of Diomedes and Odysseus, as well as of Dolon, is taken for
granted.

The Sally

Not only are the prologues to the expeditions in the two epics
quite different in detail, but also the narratives of the adventures
with all their apparent similarities, are quite distinct. To begin
with, it seems that Vergil has seized upon several undistin-
guished passages in the *Dolonia* and used them as understood

or interpreted by the scholiasts to serve as the pivots upon which the action of his plot turns.

The Exhange of Arms

As the two Greek heroes are about to set out on their adventure, Homer describes an exchange of arms on which the scholiasts comment at length, especially on the word κυνέη, used to describe the helmet Diomedes receives:

Κ 258: ἡ διπλῆ, ὅτι "κυνέην" μὲν καταχρηστικῶς τὴν ἐκ ταυρείου δέρματος, "ἄφαλον δὲ καὶ ἄλοφον" κατ᾽ ἐπιτήδευσιν, ἵνα λανθάνει · φάλοι γὰρ τὰ ἐπὶ τῶν περικεφαλαίων λαμπρὰ ἀσπιδίσκια, λόφοι δὲ αἱ τριχώσεις. [A] ἄλοφον) πρὸς τὸ λανθάνειν. [T]

Note that the "helmet" [lit., "dog's skin"] serves here as the word for a helmet of bull's hide, and without "horn" [ornamentation] and crest for a special purpose, so that he could go without detection. For "horns" are the bright little disks on helmets and the crests are made of hair. without crest) to escape detection.

Even the famed boar's tusk helmet donned by Odysseus was interpreted as having been for protection rather than ornamentation:

Κ 259: ῥύεται δὲ κάρη) δείκνυσιν ὅτι πρὸς μόνον σκέπην, οὐ πρὸς κόσμον πεποίηται, ὥστε τῇ μὲν ἐμπλοκῇ τῶν ἱμάντων δυσδιάλυτον εἶναι τὸ κράνος, τὴν δὲ ἔξωθεν ἐπιφάνειαν σκέπεσθαι μετὰ τῶν ὀδόντων πυκνῶς ἐρεισθέντων. [BT]
Κ 262 : ῥινοῦ ποιητήν) πρὸς τὸ λαθεῖν τὴν περικεφαλαίαν. [A]

And guards the heads) He shows that it was made for protection, alone, not for ornamentation, so that the helmet is hard to shatter because of the meshwork of leather thongs and the exterior surface protects as well, with the teeth firmly implanted.
Made of leather) The helmet's purpose is to escape detection.

Meriones' gift of the bow was also seen in the same light:

Κ 260: Μηριόνης δ᾽ Ὀδυσῆι δίδου βιόν) ὡς Κρὴς ἔχει τόξον, ὅπως βάλλῃ λανθάνων τοὺς ἐν φωτί. . . .[T]

While Meriones gave Odysseus a bow) Just as a Cretan has
a bow to shoot at those in the light while escaping notice. . . .

The description of the arms, to the ancient commentators at
least, appears to have indicated a strong concern to escape
detection. Diomedes, moreover, like Agamemnon, is already
clad in the hide of an animal.[18]

A similar exchange of armor takes place in the *Aeneid*.
We are told nothing of Euryalus's attire, but we are informed
that Nisus received a lion pelt from Mnestheus and that Aletes
exchanged (or changed) helmets with him (306–7):

> dat Niso Mnestheus pellem horrentisque leonis
> exuvias, galeam fidus permutat Aletes.

On the use of the word *galea* Servius remarked (*ad Aen.* IX. 307):

> galeae enim sunt explorantum, sicut etiam Homerus os-
> tendit.[19]

This may well be an example of Servius's practice of appropriating comments from the Homeric scholia, but in this case
it is very doubtful if it was without regard for the significance
of the comment for the particular passage in the *Aeneid*, especially in view of the ensuing action.

Time and Peripety

At the conclusion of the Greek council, and just before the
exchange of armor, Odysseus says to Diomedes (X. 251–53):

> "But let us go: for the night draws far along, and the dawn
> nears,
> the stars have gone far on their course, and the full of the
> night has passed by,
> through two portions, and the third portion is that which
> is left to us."

The scholiasts commented in great detail on this passage,
especially the last line, which was athetized:

> K 251 : μάλα γὰρ νὺξ ἄνεται) ἤδη πρὸ τῆς ἐξόδου περὶ
> τοῦ καιροῦ συμβουλεύει, κατεπείγων αὐτόν · ἄτοπον γὰρ
> πρὸς ἠῶ κατασκόπους πέμπεσθαι. δεόντως οὖν αὐτὸν
> εἵλετο. [BT][20]

The night draws far along) Immediately before their departure he gives advice concerning the critical time, urging him on, for it is unfitting to send spies out towards dawn. Fittingly, then, he takes him.

The comment that it is unfitting to send out spies towards dawn is of no real consequence for the plot of the *Dolonia*, and Odysseus's words at this juncture seem only to serve to hasten their departure and so provide a suspenseful transition to the action of the expedition itself.

A bit later as Odysseus and Diomedes are making their way toward the Trojan encampment, they become aware of someone approaching them from the opposite direction (339–40):

he [Dolon] went on his way, eagerly, but illustrious Odysseus
was aware of him coming. . . .

A scholiast wondered how Odysseus could "see" so much:

K 339: φράσατο) ὡς προνοῶν μὴ καὶ παρὰ τῶν πολεμίων εἴη τις δόλος · ὁ δὲ Διομήδης, ὡς καταφρονῶν τῶν κινδύνων καὶ μέγα τι θέλων διαπράξασθαι τοὺς πολεμίους, οὐ προνοεῖ. [BT]
πῶς δὲ τὸν ἐρωδιὸν μὴ ὁρῶντες αὐτὸν ὁρῶσιν ; ἴσως ὅτι πρὸς ὄρθρον ἢ σελήνη ἀνέσχεν. [B][21]

Was aware) As taking precautions lest there be some treachery from the enemy, but Diomedes, disdainful of the danger, since he was intent on accomplishing some great [deed] against the enemy, takes no precaution. [BT] How do they see him when they did not see the heron (275)? Probably because towards dawn the moon arose. [B]

There is, however, no mention of the "moon rising towards dawn" in the *Dolonia*, nor is there any mention of the moon at all.[22] We shall see, on the other hand, in what way Vergil turned this foreboding hour just before dawn to dramatic use, and how the outcome of the entire episode is made to hinge upon it.

The exploits of Diomedes and Odysseus in the camp of the sleeping Thracians are brought to a close in the following manner. Diomedes is in the midst of destroying the enemy when Odysseus, as he loosens the horses of Rhesus, whistles to him (503–11):

But he waited, divided in his mind as to what he would best
do,
whether to seize the chariot, wherein lay the bright armor,
and draw it away by the pole, or lift it and carry it off
with him,
or strip the life from still more of the Thracians. Meanwhile
as he was pondering all this in his heart, Athene
came and stood beside him, and spoke to great Diomedes:
"Think now, son of great-hearted Tydeus, of getting back
to the hollow ships; else you might go back with men pursuing
if there should be some other god to waken the Trojans."[23]

The scholiasts comment on the scene as follows:

K 503: αὐτὰρ ὁ μερμήριζε) φιλότιμος γὰρ ὢν καὶ νέος
δυσαπαλλάκτως εἶχε τοῦ εὑρήματος. [BT]

Divided in his mind) Being eager for honor and young, it
was difficult for him to draw away from his "windfall."

On Athena's admontion to Diomedes and the need for her
intervention at this point, they continue:

K 509: νόστου δὴ μνῆσαι) ὅτι δεῖ μάλιστα ἐν ταῖς εὐτυχίαις τὸ μέλλον σκοπεῖν καὶ μὴ ἀπλήστως χρῆσθαι ταῖς
εὐτυχίας. ὅτι δὲ τοῦτον εἶχεν Ὀδυσσεὺς τὸν νοῦν, δῆλον
διὰ τοῦ "ῥοίζησεν δ' ἄρα πιφαύσκων Διομήδει" (502) . . . .
[BT]

"Think now of getting back") [Note?] that it is necessary
especially in [times of] good fortune to look out for what
is to come and not to use one's good luck with insatiable
desire. It is apparent that Odysseus has this sense from the
fact that "He whistled to brilliant Diomedes as a signal to
him" (502).

With the aid of Athena's warning, the Greek pair safely return
to their camp.[24]

    A careful reading of the Nisus-Euryalus adventure reveals
that at the time the action first begins, night is not very far
advanced. Enough time has elapsed, however, for the campfires of the Rutulians to have died down and for the enemy
to have become drowsy with drink.[25] Somewhat later, after
the young Trojans have left their fortifications, they pass
directly into the enemy camp and at once begin to hew a bloody

path through the sleeping Rutulians.[26] Vergil has carefully made
reference again to the dying embers of the campfires (351) by
which, ostensibly, the two were able to see their way, taking
advantage of the deep shadows. There is no mention of the
moon.

Euryalus, bent on further destruction, was stealthily approaching the camp of Messapus when Nisus, suddenly struck
by their indiscriminate slaughter and mindful of their mission
to summon Aeneas, warns his friend (354–56):

> (sensit enim nimia caede atque cupidine ferri)
> "absistamus," ait, "nam lux inimica propinquat.
> poenarum exhaustum satis est, via facta per hostis."

The warning "absistamus nam lux inimica propinquat" has
rightly been compared with Odysseus's words to Diomedes as
the two were preparing to leave the Greek camp (X. 251):
"But let us go: for the night draws far along, and the dawn
nears. . . ." These words in the *Aeneid* far from merely serving
to hasten their departure, allude explicitly to a danger all too
imminently realized. The Trojan pair did not set out at a
dangerous hour; rather their eagerness for spoils had delayed
them until this very hazardous moment just before dawn.[27]

Nisus, with no need for an admonition from Athena, sees
the danger and warns his friend. His thought at the moment,
"sensit enim nimia caede atque cupidine ferri," and warning,
"poenarum exhaustum satis est . . ." is virtually the same as the
scholiast's comment (BT 509): "and not to make use of good
fortune with insatiate desire" (καὶ μὴ ἀπλήστως χρῆσθαι
ταῖς εὐτυχίαις). Euryalus, on the other hand, to paraphrase
scholium BT on 503, in his youthful eagerness for honor (φιλότιμος γὰρ ὢν καὶ νέος), does not easily relinquish his opportunity to gain more spoils (δυσαπαλλάκτως ἔχει τοῦ εὐρή-
ματος) and at once snatches up various pieces of armor (365–
66):

> tum galeam Messapi habilem cristisque decoram
> induit. . . .

On this line, Servius comments (*ad Aen.* IX. 365):

> cristisque decoram: bene praemittit dicens 'decoram'; nam
> eius splendore prodente Euryalus capitur. . . .[28]

At this very moment, a squadron of Latin cavalry rides up: the
horsemen suddenly see the gleam of light reflected by Euryalus's stolen helmet (373–74):

> et galea Euryalum sublustri noctis in umbra
> prodidit immemorem radiisque adversa refulsit.

Servius's comment is again noteworthy (*ad Aen.* IX. 373):

> sublustri noctis: sublustris nox est habens aliquid lucis.
> 374: radiis: lunaribus intelligendum.

Servius's remark, unlike that of scholium K 339 concerning the
moon, is based upon a "fact" which Vergil has carefully prepared for: Nisus, realizing that Euryalus has been captured,
turns towards the moon and prays for aid from the very source
which has betrayed his friend (403). The hour is shortly before
dawn.

For the peripety of the Nisus-Euryalus episode, the question
of darkness and light is crucial. Their fate is sealed by the
reflection of the moon glancing off the decoration of the plundered helmet. The two young heroes are captured and put to
death and accordingly pay the penalty for their excessive lust
for spoils and resultant lack of caution.

Motivation of the Action

There remains one more consideration of the external construction in the scholia from which Vergil may very well also have
benefitted. The motivation for the expedition of the Greek
warriors seems forgotten in the description of their exploits.
To the casual reader the excitement of the account more than
justifies the inclusion of the episode, but it should be remembered that the original intention of Nestor was to learn the
plans of the Trojans for the coming day.[29] Interrogating Dolon
after his capture, Odysseus says (405 ff.):

> "But come, tell me this thing and recite it to me accurately.
> Where did you leave Hektor, the people's shepherd, when
> you came here?

Where is his gear of war lying? Where are his horses?
How are the rest of the Trojans disposed, the guards and
the sleepers?"

then repeats three lines of Nestor's speech (208–10):

"What do they deliberate among themselves? Do they
purpose
to stay where they are, close to the ships? Or else to with-
draw back
into the city, now that they have beaten the Achaians?"

These three lines were athetized by Aristarchus:

K 409: ... ὅτι ἐκ τῶν τοῦ Νέστορος λόγων μετενηνεγμένοι
εἰσὶν οὐ δεόντως. γελοῖος γὰρ ἔσται ὁ Ὀδυσσεύς, ἤδη
τῆς ὥρας προκεκοφυίας, ἐρωτῶν εἰ μένουσιν ἢ ἀπέρχονται
ἐπὶ τὴν πόλιν. καὶ ὡς ἂν τούτων μὴ εἰρημένων ὁ Δόλων
πρὸς μὲν τὰ ἄλλα ἀποκρίνεται, πρὸς δὲ ταῦτα οὔ. ... [A]

.... because [these lines] have been transferred from Nestor's speech, and not fittingly; for Odysseus is absurd—with
the hour already advanced—asking if they remain or are
going back to the city. And as though these words had
not been said, Dolon answers to the rest, but not to these
[questions].

Two objections appear to have been raised: (1) that the information sought would have been acquired too late to have
been of any advantage, and (2) that Dolon, never makes a
reply to the inquiry of the purpose for which the expedition
was made.

Regardless of what we may think of the scholiast's objections, the fact remains that the primary reason for the venture
appears to have been overlooked by the Greek heroes in their
eagerness for plunder. At any rate, they were unsuccessful
in their reconnaissance of the enemy and, if the lines in question
actually were later interpolations, the reason would surely have
been to refocus the reader's attention on the original purpose
of the expedition, and presumably because Homer seemed to
have ignored it in the course of his narrative.

This is not the case in the *Aeneid*. Nisus and Euryalus do
indeed lose sight of their mission, and for the same reason as
do Odysseus and Diomedes. For the Trojan pair, however,

their eagerness for booty becomes the temporary but decisive dereliction of duty which results in failure and death.

There is one more further implication in the scholiast's remark that the information, if acquired, would have been gained too late to have been of any strategic value. If indeed Duckworth is correct in his belief that the mission of Nisus and Euryalus was undertaken after Aeneas had already left Pallanteum, and that accordingly their venture was doomed to failure even before it began, the impact of this ancient criticism of the *Dolonia* would take on still another dimension.[30]

Thus it is that Vergil has seized upon three relatively unimportant points of the plot of the *Dolonia* and woven them into a network of attendant circumstances which are combined in such a way as to bring about the downfall of Nisus and Euryalus. In each case, the seeds of the plot as it was developed by Vergil seem to have been sown first by the ancient commentators on Homer:

a) The foresight of the Greek pair in choosing inconspicuous armor, and especially the helmet without crest and "bright studs" (cf. scholia on K 258–59 and Servius *ad Aen.* IX. 307), is sharply contrasted with Euryalus's lack of caution (*immemorem*, l. 373) in donning the crested helmet of Messapus (365).[31]

b) The question of time, the hours just before dawn (scholium on K 251), and of the moon which Homer never mentions (scholia on K 276 and 339) is of little consequence in the *Dolonia*, for the threat of danger arising because of the hour never does materialize in the *Iliad*. Odysseus's words, moreover, concerning the approach of dawn, which serve only to hasten the spies out on their mission, have been effectively transposed by Vergil to the danger which Nisus suddenly realizes and is presently all too real. In the *Aeneid*, therefore, the rising of the moon at this very moment in combination with the flashing of the crested helmet is the all important crux on which the peripety of the action turns.

c) In the *Dolonia*, Aristarchus regarded the purpose of the mission as pointless (K 409) because of the lateness of the hour (K 251), and as a result, the motivation of the action appeared faulty. The purpose of the mission may rightly be overlooked in the *Iliad*, if indeed it was, but in the *Aeneid* such dereliction of duty on the part of protagonists is the cause of both their failure and deaths. The purpose of the mission, therefore, is never forgotten; it is of paramount importance.

Vergil would therefore appear to have extracted the implications of each of these three criticisms for his own purpose in a superb combination of Homeric factors to provide the pivot upon which the external action of the Nisus-Euryalus episode turns. It is just these three points of departure from the *Dolonia* which lead directly to the downfall of the Trojan heroes that cause this episode of the *Aeneid* to seem at the same time so very similar, yet so entirely different from Homer's version.

CHARACTER

The characterization of the two Trojan warriors, whom Vergil has chosen to portray as close friends rather than as companions or "accomplices," as if in answer to the comment of the scholiast (K 242), is in its own way no less Homeric than the external structure of the plot. Reference has already been made to Homer's description of Diomedes while he was "divided in his mind as to what he would best do" (503: ὅ τι κύντατον ἔρδοι) after Odysseus had whistled to him as a signal to return to the safety of the camp, and to the scholiast's comment that inasmuch as he is young and eager, it is difficult for him to give up his "windfall" (K 509). Homer's description of Diomedes while he is slaughtering the sleeping Thracians, is verbally quite reminiscent of Nisus's thoughts as he looks out over the plain from his watch at the opening of the episode and tells his friend of his desire (186–87):

> "aut pugnam aut aliquid iamdudum invadere magnum mens agitat mihi. . . ."

To be sure, Homer does not portray Diomedes in such finely drawn lines as Vergil does his heroes, but it is clear from the scholiasts' observations on Diomedes' actions that Vergil has framed his characterization of Nisus and Euryalus in the same light.

In the course of his description of Nisus as he kills the sleeping Latins, Vergil employs a simile of a lion even as Homer does to describe Diomedes as he wreaks havoc among the sleeping Thracians (*Il.* X. 485–87):

> As a lion advancing on the helpless herds unshepherded
> of sheep or goats pounces upon them with wicked intention,
> so the son of Tydeus attacked the Thracian people. . . .

Aen. IX. 339–41:

> impastus ceu plena leo per ovilia turbans
> (suadet enim vesana fames) manditque trahitque
> molle pecus mutumque metu, fremit ore cruento. . . .

We will note two primary differences: the Trojan lion is portrayed as having been goaded on by an insane hunger and as roaring out of his bloody jaws.

Reference has already been made to the many recent studies which demonstrate that the Vergilian simile often applies not merely to the external, "visual" act, but as well to the inner, psychic, or "spiritual" condition of the figure which is compared. We have also seen that similar appreciations of Homeric similes are frequently preserved in the scholia, especially on similes which liken a warrior to a lion.[32] With this in view, let us reexamine the first such simile of the *Iliad*, which is not unlike the one that Vergil has adapted from the *Dolonia*. Here again, the lion is a hungry one (*Il.* III. 23–28):

> . . . he was glad, like a lion who comes on a mighty carcass,
> in his hunger chancing upon the body of a horned stag
> or wild goat; who eats it eagerly, although against him
> are hastening the hounds in their speed and the stalwart
>   young men:
> thus Menelaus was happy finding godlike Alexandros. . . .

The scholiast comments in part:

> Γ 25: εἴπερ ἂν αὐτὸν σεύωνται) ὥσπερ οὖν λέοντα παρο-
> ξύνει λιμὸς εἰς ἀπερίσκεπτον κίνδυνον, οὕτω καὶ νέον
> ἄνδρα πολεμίου ζῆλος εἰς ἀνεκλόγιστον ἀγῶνα προτρέ-
> πεται. [ABT]

Although against him are hastening) Just as its hunger spurs
the lion on to run into an unforeseen risk, so does a young
man's eagerness for war urge him on into an unreasoned
[struggle] act.

This is precisely the implication of the Vergilian simile: the
lion is *impastus*: he is goaded on by *vesana fames*. Perhaps,
too, it would not be too extravagant to suggest that this insane
hunger, or lust, is the equivalent of *dira cupido*.[33] At any rate,
in his youthful hunger/desire for the glory of some great deed
(cf. also *Aen.* IX. 184 ff. and *Il.* X. 503 ff.), Nisus has embarked
not only on a dangerous mission, but has indulged as well in
a wanton and unreasoned act of slaughter (ἀνεκλόγιστος ἀγών)
and disregarded the danger which was soon to befall them
ἀπερίσκεπτος κίνδυνος). We should, once more, recall the words
of the scholiast which comment upon Diomedes in exactly the
same situation (K 503), "Being eager for honor and young, it'
is difficult for him to draw away from his 'windfall'."[34] Again,
this is precisely the situation in the *Aeneid* and exactly how
Vergil chose to characterize Nisus and Euryalus.

This particular simile has still further significance within
the total framework of the *Aeneid*. The phrase, *fremit ore
cruento*, is used first in the *Aeneid* to describe the demonic
Impius Furor in Jupiter's prophecy of the future grandeur of
Rome (I. 296), and again in a lion simile used to characterize
Turnus at the very opening of the last book of the *Aeneid*.
Here, as well as in its other occurrences, it is clearly symbolic
of the madness and fury of men in war. The other addition to
the Homeric simile is no less symbolic. The phrase, *suadet enim
vesana fames*, is reminiscent of another demon, one of many
which haunt the gates of the underworld, *malesuada Fames*
(VI. 276).

Conclusion

It is due, then, to the young Trojans' overzealous quest for
spoils and glory together with their lack of caution that they
were blinded to the real purpose of their mission and led to

an untimely and pathetic destruction. It was their own character and not the gods that sealed their fate.[35] In retrospect the words of Aletes to the pair when they first approach him in council sound an ominous and ironic note (IX. 252–55):

> "quae vobis, quae digna, viri, pro laudibus istis
> praemia posse rear solvi? pulcherrima primum
> di moresque dabunt vestri: tum cetera reddet
> actutum pius Aeneas. . . ."

And as if to emphasize the irony still further, Vergil describes Euryalus as he piteously attempts to escape the Latin cavalry, hindered as he was by the booty with which he was burdened (384 f.):

> Euryalum tenebrae ramorum onerosaque praeda
> impediunt. . . .

This is an ironic echo of their confidence in success as they first take leave of the Trojan camp (242 f.):

> "mox hic cum spoliis ingenti caede peracta
> adfore cernetis. . . ."

We need only recall the words of Jupiter in the book which immediately follows (X. 111–13):

> ". . . sua cuique exorsa laborem
> fortunamque ferent. rex Iuppiter omnibus idem.
> fata viam invenient."

Several years ago, Duckworth pointed out that nowhere in this episode of the *Aeneid* do the gods appear.[36] This is quite in contrast to the action of the *Dolonia*, which is not only sanctioned with an omen by Athena (274 ff.) as the pair first make their way onto the deserted battlefield, but is also safely brought to its conclusion by the direct intervention of the same goddess (509 ff.).

It is well known that the scholiasts frequently equate Athena with "reason," but in this episode the use of "reason" is much more than a mere inversion of poetic convention. The original question of Nisus, with which the tale opens (184 ff.):

> ". . . dine hunc ardorem mentibus addunt,
> Euryale, an sua cuique deus fit dira cupido?

aut pugnam aut aliquid iamdudum invadere magnum
mens agitat mihi, nec placida contenta quiete est."

is answered in death. It is just this question which so distinguishes the Vergilian episode from the Homeric.

As it stands, the *Dolonia* is an exciting adventure, told for its own interest and concluded to the advantage of the Greeks. The climax of this tale in the *Aeneid* is not to be found in the *Iliad*, nor is it intimated in the scholia, nor are the pathos and intricate interplay and development of the action as a whole included. What is extant in the scholia, however, are the traditional criticisms of the want of realistic motivation for the action because of the lateness of the hour, and the exegesis of speeches, similes, characterization, and even the choice of armor. In each of these points, Vergil seems to have been well aware of the ancient commentaries and to have carefully considered them in his adaptation of this episode. Frequently as we have seen, the variations upon the basic theme of the *Dolonia* appear to have been anticipated in the scholia.[37]

VI

The Twelfth Book of the Aeneid

The twelfth book of the *Aeneid* is generally regarded as being
the most "Homeric" of the Vergilian epic: the reader is immediately reminded of two cardinal scenes in the *Iliad*, the
breaking of the truce (*Il.* IV) and the duel between Hector and
Achilles (*Il.* XXII), in addition to various incidents and images
drawn from other books. *Aeneid* XII is indeed a veritable
mosaic of Homeric passages and stands as a remarkable tribute
to Vergil's assimilative powers. This book abounds in opportunities for the student interested in comparing the Homeric
with the later "literary epic" represented by the *Aeneid*.

Confronted with the remarkable resemblances of sub-
stantial portions of this climactic book of the *Aeneid* to parallel
episodes in the *Iliad* and the equally remarkable departures in
detail from the original source, we should expect in this book
to discover still more indications of Vergil's responsiveness
to his literary inheritance, especially in view of the relative
wealth of ancient commentary extant on *Iliad* IV and XXII.
Let us begin with a brief passage which occurs the night before
the swearing of the oaths.

After Achilles has received the armor made by Hephaestus and has been partially reconciled with Agamemnon, the
Greeks prepare to renew their conflict with the Trojans. At
this point Homer presents us with an unusual scene of Achilles
arming himself in the midst of the Achaean hosts (*Il.* XIX.
362–68):

The shining swept to the sky and all the earth was laughing
about them
under the glitter of bronze and beneath their feet stirred
the thunder
of men, within whose midst brilliant Achilleus helmed him.
A clash went from the grinding of his teeth, and his eyes
glowed
as if they were the stare of a fire, and the heart inside him
was entered with sorrow beyond endurance. Raging at the
Trojans
he put on the gifts of the god, that Hephaistos wrought him
with much toil.

A typically detailed description of the various pieces of armor
follows. The scholia comment:

T 365: τοῦ καὶ ὀδόντων μέν) ἀθετοῦνται στίχοι τέσσαρες
(365–68) · γελοῖον γὰρ τὸ βρυχᾶσθαι τὸν 'Αχιλλέα, ἥ τε
συνέπεια οὐδὲν ζητεῖ διαγραφέντων αὐτῶν. ὁ δὲ Σιδώ-
νιος ἠθετηκέναι μὲν τὸ πρῶτόν φησιν αὐτοὺς τοὺς ἀρι-
θμούς (αὐτοὺς τὸν 'Αρίσταρχον, Bekker), ὕστερον δὲ πε-
ριελεῖν τοὺς ὀβελούς, ποιητικὸν νομίσαντα τὸ τοιοῦτο.
ὁ μέντοι 'Αμμώνιος ἐν τῷ περὶ τῆς ἐπεκδοθείσης διορ-
θώσεως οὐδὲν τοιοῦτο λέγει, διπλῆν δὲ προσθετέον τῷ
"δῦν' ἄχος ἄτλητον, ὁ δ' ἄρα Τρωσὶ μενεαίνων" (367),
ὅτι τὸ "μενεαίνων" νῦν "θυμούμενος" σημαίνει. [A]¹

From the grinding of his teeth) These four lines are athetized;
Achilles' gnashing of teeth is "grotesque" and the connection
of the verses requires none of them if removed. Sidonius,
however, says that first Aristarchus (so Bekker) athetized
them but later took away the *obeloi*, thinking the lines poetic.
Ammonius, on the other hand, in his work concerning [Aris-
tarchus's] second edition [of Homer] made no such remark
but did say that line 367 must be noted as unusual because
the word "desire eagerly" in Homer now means "be angry."

Whatever the original argument over the lines, it seems that
Aristarchus (?) ultimately thought that the description on the
whole was fitting and indeed, "poetic," doubtless as a vivid
portrayal of Achilles' rising frenzy.² On the other hand, as has
already been pointed out, such descriptions of the "emotional"
state are not common to Homeric scenes in which heroes arm
themselves.³ Perhaps these lines were originally considered sus-
pect, in part at least, for just this reason, aside from the con-

siderations specifically mentioned in the scholium. Scholium T, moreover, points directly to the portrayal of emotions, apparently with approval:

T 366: ἐν δέ οἱ ἦτορ) μετὰ τὰς τοῦ σώματος ἐκφράσεις εἶτα καὶ τῆς ψυχῆς τὴν διάθεσιν δηλοῖ.

And the heart within him was entered with sorrow) After the physical description [of his passion—so Hesychius], he then reveals the disposition of his soul.

Vergil seems clearly to have had this scene in mind when he described Turnus arming himself for battle the night before he was at last to confront Aeneas in hand to hand combat. Brandishing his spear, the already fully armed hero addressed to it a fervent prayer that it be granted to him to slay his adversary. At the conclusion of his prayer, Vergil adds (*Aen.* XII. 101–2):

his agitur furiis, totoque ardentis ab ore
scintillae absistunt, oculis micat acribus ignis. . . .

The scene concludes with a simile likening Turnus to a raging bull who in his eagerness for battle paws the ground while tossing his horns in the air and charges a tree.

Appropriating the scene from Homer, Vergil has actually omitted only the gnashing of teeth which, as Heinze noted, was the element which initially offended Alexandrian taste.[4] There is one noteworthy difference in arrangement, perhaps because of Vergil's consideration of both scholia on the integration of emotions into the scene. Achilles' anguish and wrath are described as he begins to put on his armor and the enumeration of the various pieces of armor follows, detracting somewhat from the overall effect.[5] Turnus, on the other hand, first dons his armor after which the originally athetized lines are inserted. As if in rising crescendo, the scene concludes with the simile likening Turnus to a raging bull. This may well be Vergil's rendering of "and the heart inside him was entered with sorrow beyond endurance. Raging at the Trojans. . . ." (366–67).

The scene of the hero arming himself, as it stands in the *Aeneid* serves explicitly as a transition to the portrayal of Turnus's emotional furor, and with the addition of the simile

becomes the vehicle of an important feature in the characterization of the Rutulian prince. The fact that this scene was
deliberately set the night before the actual confrontation was
to take place, as Heinze noted, emphasizes this view still more.
This simple inversion of the order of the Homeric passage may
well have been prompted by the scholiasts' discussion and
criticism of this unique scene in the *Iliad*, which in the *Aeneid*
becomes crucial for an understanding of Turnus's character.

THE BREAKING OF THE TRUCE[6]

The Disguise

The shot of Tolumnius (*Aen.* XII. 266 ff.), which broke the
truce between the Trojans and the Rutulians, is based upon the
shot of Pandarus (*Il.* IV. 86 ff.), and has long been regarded as
one of the most suitable passages for a study of Vergil's imi-
tative art.[7] For the purpose of this study, the scholia on this
entire episode are among the most significant of the entire corpus.

After Aphrodite had rescued Paris from Menelaus's onslaught, Agamemnon declared his brother the victor and demanded that the terms of the pact be fulfilled. Following a
lengthy scene on Olympus, Athena, in the guise of Laodocus,
suggested to Pandarus that he shoot Menelaus and so win the
praise and gratitude of Paris and the Trojans. Of Athena's
appearance to Pandarus, Homer says only this (*Il.* IV. 86-88):

> She in the likeness of a man merged among the Trojans
> assembled,
> Laodokos, Antenor's son, a powerful spearman,
> searching for godlike Pandaros. . . .

The scholiasts discuss this choice of disguise in some detail and
their remarks again allow us to follow quite closely the critical
methods of the Alexandrians when commenting upon Homer's
poiêsis:

Δ 87: Λαοδόκῳ ᾿Αντηνορίδῃ κρατερῷ αἰχμητῇ). . . . καλῶς δὲ τούτῳ εἴκασται. ᾿Αντήνορος γὰρ ὢν παῖς καὶ

παραβὰς νόμον προξενίας καὶ τοῦτον θέλει παραβῆναι
νόμον σπονδῶν · εἰ γὰρ ἕτερος ἦν ὁ συμβουλεύων, ἔφη
ἂν ὁ Πάνδαρος, διὰ τί μὴ σὺ παραβήσῃ τοὺς ὅρκους;
[BT] εἰκότως δὲ ὁ τοῦ φιλοξένου ἀνδρὸς παῖς Λαοδόκος
καίτοι μὴ ὢν καλεῖται. ἀλλὰ καὶ κρατερὸς αἰχμητής,
ἤτοι εἰς τὸ αἰχμάζειν ἰσχυρός. [B][8]

Laodocus, Antenor's son, a powerful spearman) Well does he
like her to this man. For being the son of Antenor and trans-
gressing the law of foreign friendship, he [Athena] wishes him
to break the agreement of the treaty; for if some other person
had suggested this, he would have said, "Why don't you
transgress the oaths?" [BT] Fittingly, being the son of a
man who is "hospitable to foreigners" [in a socio-political
sense], he is called "Laodocus" ["receiving the people," or
"hospitable"] although he is not so. He is, however, also
a "powerful spearman," that is, mighty in hurling the spear
[a warrior as opposed to archer]. [B]

Briefly they point out that Homer did well to have Athena
disguise herself as Laodocus, for not only is he (as Homer says)
a mighty warrior, but he is also the son of Antenor, the πρόξενος
of the Achaeans (cf. schol. BT on *Il.* III. 206). Furthermore,
they make explicit what is only implicit in the *Iliad*: the influence of such a noble warrior as Laodocus, and one who should
know and respect agreements with foreigners, lends authority
to his treacherous suggestion that Pandarus break the truce:

Δ 95: . . . πιστὸς δὲ ὁ λόγος παρ' ἀνδρὸς λεγόμενος ἐπιφα-
νοῦς. [BT]

Trustworthy are the words of a distinguished man.

It is also pointed out in some detail that treachery is innate in
Pandarus, and his genealogy is given in support of this view.[9]
Aristotle, himself, is cited to explain why one of the allies rather
than a Trojan was chosen to commit the treacherous act: Paris
was hated by his countrymen.[10] In short, the scholiasts attempted to explain the reasons for Homer's choice of characters
in their effort to explicate the motivation of the action.

An examination of Vergil's handling of this same scene in
the *Aeneid* is in order. After the exchange of oaths between
Aeneas and Latinus, Vergil carefully describes the thoughts of

the Rutulians as they assemble to witness the ceremony and subsequent duel (216–18): we are told of their varying emotions and how they begin to pity their prince when they realize how unequal the combatants are. Turnus, unlike Paris, is esteemed by nearly all his followers throughout the *Aeneid*, and it is upon this fact that Vergil has begun to lay the grounds for the psychological motivation of his version of the breaking of the truce.[11]

As soon as she was aware of the disposition of the Rutulians, Juturna assumed the form of Camers and set out at once to break the truce in her effort to save her brother (224–26):

> in medias acies formam adsimulata Camerti
> (cui genus a proavis ingens clarumque paternae
> nomen erat virtutis, et ipse acerrimus armis).

Vergil, likewise, has chosen for Juturna a figure who is a renowned warrior of a famed and noble family, but following the exposition of the scholia, leaves no doubt as to Camers's distinction, and accordingly, Juturna's reasons for her choice of disguise. Servius comments on line 225:

> cui genus a proavis ingens: cuius auctoritatem
> commendabat et origo maiorum et paterna virtus
> et propria fortitudo.[12]

This comment, remarkably reminiscent of the scholia (especially BT on 95), would seem to indicate that Servius was also aware of the ancient commentaries on this scene of the *Iliad* and that he elucidated Juturna's disguise in the light of them.

More important, however, is the fact that Vergil has seen fit to add to his description what the scholiasts had felt was implied (though not stated) by Homer concerning Athena's choice of disguise. The addition, moreover, of the portrayal of the Rutulians' uneasy emotions makes them all the more susceptible to Juturna's proposal and so provides the psychological motivation of the action. The lack of just such motivation is what Aristotle and the scholiasts had seen as deficient, here and in the entire episode, and had consequently attempted to read into Homer's choice of characters for the breaking of the truce.

ι

The Target

In the *Iliad*, Menelaus is Pandarus's target. Scholium BT questions this choice:

Δ 100: ἀλλ᾽ ἄγ᾽ ὀΐστευσον Μενελάου) πῶς μὴ ᾽Αγαμέμνονα τοξεύει ἀκαθόπλιστον ὄντα, ἤ τινα τῶν ἀρίστων ἄλλον, ἀλλὰ τὸν ἐντεθωρακισμένον Μενέλαον ;

Come, then, let go an arrow against Menelaos) Why does he not [rather] shoot Agamemnon since he is unarmed, or some other one of the nobles, but [chooses] the armored Menelaus?

The *lysis* need not detain us here, but the question is not without merit, especially since the aim of Athena's stratagem was to break the truce (*Il.* IV. 64–67).[13] This could have been brought about more plausibly by shooting Agamemnon, or any of the Achaean nobles, who presumably would have been less fully armed while watching the duel than Menelaus: so it seemed to the scholiast.[14]

After her inflammatory speech in the guise of Camers (227–37), Juturna causes an omen to appear to further ignite the Rutulians' and the Latins' smouldering resentment over the duel (238–40). The omen is fittingly interpreted by the augur Tolumnius as a heaven-sent sign for them to come to the aid of their prince. He immediately hurls his spear at the Trojan throng while those about him prepare for battle. The spear, aimed at no one in particular, by chance (*forte*, 270), strikes one of nine brothers who are standing together. Griefstricken and enraged at his death, they rush blindly towards the Rutulians (271–79).[15] The motivation for the renewal of hostilities is now complete.[16]

Rather than Aeneas, who like Menelaus is harnessed in full battle array, Vergil has chosen one of the spectators of the duel as the victim of the treacherous shot which breaks the truce. The development of the action in this scene is considerably different from that of the *Iliad* and is a tribute to Vergil's poetic skill, but it will be noted that the point of departure, here as well as in the first instance, coincides with the passage criticized by the scholiasts on the *Iliad*, and again, their suggestion has been incorporated into the *Aeneid*, this time to serve as a cardinal point upon which the action of this episode turns.

The Attack

Continuing with the sequence of the action in the *Iliad*: Menelaus is struck by Pandarus's arrow, and while he is being cared for, the Trojans suddenly and *en masse* attack the Greeks (*Il.* IV. 220 ff.). The scholiasts, pointing out the obvious want of motivation for the attack, raised the following questions:

> *Δ* 221: τόφρα δ' ἐπὶ Τρώων στίχες) διὰ τί οἱ Τρῶες, εἴπερ
> <πάλαι[B]> καταθέσθαι τὸν πόλεμον ἐβούλοντο, οὐκ
> ἐζήτουν τὸν βαλόντα, ἀλλ' εὐθὺς ὁρμῶσιν ἐπὶ τὰ ὅπλα;
> ... .πῶς δὲ πάλιν ὁ ῞Εκτωρ οὐκ ἐζήτησε τὸν βαλόντα ... ;
> [BT][17]

> All this time came on the ranks of the Trojans) Why is it that the Trojans, if they were [for a long time] desiring peace, immediately rush to arms rather than attempt to seek out the one who had shot the arrow? ... Why, in particular, does Hector not do this?

Aeneas, quite in contrast to Hector or Agamemnon, tries desperately, though in vain, to restrain his men from engaging in combat and thereby breaking the truce until he himself is treacherously wounded by an arrow (XII. 311 ff.). Like Hector, it is Turnus who disregards the terms of the truce. He makes no effort to stem the outbreak of hostilities, but rather, immediately leaps to his horse, his hopes revived, and rides "like Mars," dealing death and destruction to his helpless foe (324 ff.). This striking contrast of character revealed by the actions of both Turnus and the *pius Aeneas* (311) is surely intentional and is fundamental to an understanding of the *Aeneid*.[18]

As if in answer to both questions of the scholiasts, Vergil has thus presented us with a carefully contrived and detailed picture of the Rutulians and Latins turning away from the originally welcomed truce (cf. *Aen.* XII. 1–4) and of their growing eagerness to renew the conflict.[19] When one of the onlookers has been slain by the act of treachery, Aeneas makes every effort to uphold the terms of the peace. In both these instances Vergil has departed from the Homeric narrative precisely where the ancient commentators had criticized the lack of motivation for the action as it unfolds. More important and significant is the fact that in both these cases Vergil has developed his departures exactly along the lines implied and suggested in the Homeric scholia.

In all three variations from *Iliad* IV thus far discussed, we can clearly see how Vergil has assimilated the comments in the scholia and turned them to advantage in the finer psychological motivation and greater credibility thereby achieved. The means by which Vergil accomplished this is a remarkable tribute to his own originality and poetic artistry, both of which are set off in high relief when compared to the stark and linear conception of *Iliad* IV.

The Wounded

The excitement and concern of the Greeks around the wounded Menelaus is described at considerable length, though Homer has told us that he was only grazed by Pandarus's arrow (IV. 139). After a long address by Agamemnon who believes that his brother has been mortally wounded (148–82), Menelaus finally reassures him that this is not the case (184–86):

> "Do not fear, nor yet make afraid the Achaian people.
> The sharp arrow is not stuck in a mortal place, but the shining
> war belt turned it aside from its course, and the flap beneath it. . . ."

The scholiasts comment to the effect that Menelaus is acting like a "sick child" attempting to reassure his parents, and add that it was out of place for him to act so "softly," or "effeminately," with all the concern about him:

> *Δ* 184: θάρσει) τοιοῦτός ἐστιν, ὡσεὶ νοσῶν υἱὸς παραμυ-
> θοῖτο γονεῖς. ἄτοπος δὲ ἦν μαλθακευόμενος Μενέλαος
> ἐκείνων τὸ πάθος οἰκειουμένων. [B] (ἐκείνων οἰκειουμέ-
> νων τὴν αἰτίαν τοῦ θανάτου αὐτοῦ [T] and Erbse)

"Do not fear") He is like a sick child who would reassure his parents. It is unfitting for Menelaus to act so softly with those having sympathy for his suffering [B] (the cause of his death). [T]

The portrayal of Aeneas is exactly the opposite. After he has been wounded and is being helped back from the heat of battle, Aeneas struggles furiously to tear the arrow from his wound, and even suggests that it be cut out if necessary, so that he can immediately return to combat (387 ff.). There can be no accusation that Aeneas is "soft," or, indeed, "effeminate."

It goes without saying that Vergil would have realized that Menelaus's conduct was "unbecoming" to a king and champion of his people without the need for a scholiast to tell him. The observation is an obvious one and surely common knowledge, but it is herein that its very importance lies: Vergil *wanted* to contrast his handling of this scene with that of Homer and the character of Aeneas with that of Menelaus. Vergil expected and assumed a thorough knowledge of Homer in his readers, and without such a knowledge, much of the artistry and significance of the *Aeneid* is lost.[20]

In this respect the Servian commentary provides us with an interesting observation on this scene, specifically where Aeneas strives desperately to tear the arrow from his wound (*ad Aen.* XII. 387):

saevit: scilicet, quia non potest in bella procedere: vel quod abstractus a bellis sit. et bene viro forti servat dignitatem, qui nihil molliter facit in tam aspero vulnero: nam ideo 'infracta luctatur harundine.'

Surely the words . . . *nihil molliter facit* answer the scholiasts' μαλθακευόμενος used to describe Menelaus, and allude to the contrast of character that Vergil certainly intended between the Spartan king and Aeneas. Otherwise, Servius's comment would have little point.

The Physician

After he has been reassured by his brother, Agamemnon turns to his herald Talthybius and orders him to summon Machaon, the physician (*Il.* IV. 193–97):

"Talthybios, with all speed go call hither Machaon,
a man who is son of Asklepios and a blameless physician,
so that he may look at Menelaos, the warlike son of
Atreus, whom someone skilled in the bow's use shot with an
                                                    arrow,
Trojan or Lykian: glory to him but to us a sorrow."

Aristarchus(?) commented that line 195 (and presumably the
rest of the address) was unnecessary, since the herald can see
the need for a physician:[21]

Δ 195: ὄφρα ἴδῃ Μενέλαον) ὁ ἀστερίσκος καὶ ὀβελός,
ὅτι νῦν παρέλκει · ὁρᾷ γὰρ ὁ κῆρυξ τὴν χρείαν τοῦ Μα-
χάονος. . . . [A][22] θορυβούμενος πέρα τοῦ δέοντος φέρεται.
οὐ περιττὸς οὖν ὁ στίχος τὸ "ὅν τις ὀϊστεύσας" (196),
μιμούμενος τὸ ἦθος τῶν τεταραγμένων. [BT]

So that he may look at Menelaos) Athetized because re-
peated wrongly, since here it is extraneous; for the herald
sees the need for Machaon. . . . [A] Disturbed, he is "carried
away" beyond what is necessary. Therefore line 196 is not
excessive since it imitates the disposition of those who have
been [deeply] troubled. [BT]

In such an emergency details are unnecessary and serve only
to delay or weaken the continuity of the action.[23]

While Aeneas is being helped back to the camp by his
attendants, he struggles to extricate the arrow, as we have seen,
in his effort to return without delay to the battle now raging
about him. Vergil continues his narrative (391): "iamque aderat
Phoebo ante alios dilectus Iapyx. . . ." *Iamque aderat* is most
emphatic: Iapyx is immediately present, and of his own accord.[24]
Even as Aristarchus could see no need for details in a command
given in such an emergency, so, too, Vergil could see no need
for an awkward relay of summons: it is the physician himself
who sees the need for his services. Therefore, in the course of
an interlude in the action, while the wound is being tended to,
is the place to give the physician's medical "qualifications."

This is a very minor deviation from Homer's narrative, but
here again we can compare Vergil's skill in the *agôn* with Homer.
The awkward relay of summons for Machaon is contrasted with
Iapyx's ready awareness of the need; Menelaus's calm reas-

surance in his delayed reply to Agamemnon's solicitude and Aeneas's fiery spirit and determination are even more powerfully contrasted in Vergil's wonderfully expressed tableau. In both instances the scholiasts' criticisms and comments once more mark the points of departure for Vergil's *retractatio* of this scene in the *Iliad*.

In each of the five cases of imitation discussed, Vergil has developed the action of the *Aeneid* very carefully to avoid precisely the grounds of the scholiasts' criticisms. Granted that Vergil would obviously have been more than competent enough to see these flaws for himself, yet in this brief episode (*Aen.* XII. 216–467), so closely based upon Homer, we note that in all five variations from *Iliad* IV. 86–222, not only does the way towards Vergil's final development of the episode seem to have been indicated in the scholiasts' criticisms, but Vergil, in his endeavor to "compete" with Homer, and to further his own artistic ends, has incorporated their suggestions directly into his departures from *Iliad* IV.

THE DUEL

After Aeneas has been miraculously healed by Iapyx with the aid of Venus, he briefly addresses Ascanius and rushes off to battle in search of Turnus (*Aen.* XII. 441 ff.). The Rutulians are quickly put to flight. Still seeking only Turnus, who is kept far from his path by Juturna disguised now as the charioteer Metiscus, Aeneas roams the battlefield crying aloud for his opponent, until he is attacked by Messapus. Invoking Jupiter as his witness that the truce has been broken, now, and only now, he turns with vengeance upon any of the hapless foes who encounter him. At this point Vergil presents us with an account of the exploits of both heroes (500 ff.). Aeneas, still seeking Turnus (557), is suddenly prompted by Venus to attack Laurentum. We may now turn to an examination of the climax of the *Aeneid*, the duel between Turnus and Aeneas, and the episode of *Iliad* XXII upon which it is so closely based, the duel between

Hector and Achilles. In no other episode has Vergil's debt to Homer been so widely acknowledged.

The Attack on the City

Towards the end of *Iliad* XXI, Homer tells us that the Trojans, overwhelmed and terrified by the onslaught of Achilles, fled to seek safety within the walls of the city. During this time Achilles pursues Apollo who has taken on the guise of Agenor and is led ever farther from Troy (*Il.* XXI. 599 ff.). When he becomes aware of Apollo's ruse, Achilles speeds towards Troy before whose gates stands Hector, alone and now resolved to await his enemy (XXII. 36). At this point the scholiasts wondered why no one attempted to do battle with Hector. In other words, Homer fails to account for the whereabouts of the rest of the Achaeans:

> X 36: Ἀχιλῆϊ μάχεσθαι) ἄξιον ζητήσεως πῶς ἀπόντος Ἀχιλλέως μηδεὶς πολεμεῖ Ἕκτορι. ἢ τάχα συνεπο-
> ρεύοντο αὐτῷ καὶ οἱ λοιποὶ ἀριστεῖς διώκοντι Ἀπόλ-
> λωνα. Μεγακλείδης δέ φησι ταῦτα πάντα πλάσματα
> εἶναι. [B][25]

> To fight with Achilles) This is a worthy question: Why does no one fight with Hector in the absence of Achilles? [. . .?] Or because the rest of the nobles proceed with Achilles as he pursues Apollo. Megacleides, however, says that all this [the duel, or *monomachia* of Achilles] is unrealistically constructed.

The "problem," if minor, has not been raised without some reason; the scholiast has pointed out a well-known "weakness" in Homer's narrative technique, his apparent inability to portray simultaneous action.[26] We know only that the Achaeans came near the walls of Troy (XXII, 1–6), but beyond that the situation remains somewhat puzzling.

The circumstances in the *Aeneid* are totally different, and at no point can the problem raised by Megacleides and the later scholiast be raised of the action of Book XII; we never lose sight of the Trojans, or of Turnus, who at this juncture is described as sluggishly pursuing a few stragglers at the far end of the battlefield (614–16). Vergil was without doubt not so struck by the "weakness" of Homer's narrative technique as he was intent on the development and contrast of his complexly detailed characterizations of both Turnus and Aeneas within the loose, general framework of the Homeric episode. He was also well aware of the Homeric criticism both here and in the ensuing action.[27] It will be recalled that Aeneas, frustrated in his effort to find Turnus, is suddenly prompted to turn his attack toward Laurentum.[28] He immediately summons the Trojan leaders together and orders them to direct their forces in an attempt to storm the city. This speech fills the gap of *Iliad* XXII and also serves clearly to illuminate Turnus's irresponsibility in his failure to honor the treaty. Aeneas concludes his address (570–73):

> "scilicet exspectem libeat dum proelia Turno
> nostra pati rursusque velit concurrere victus?
> hoc caput, o cives, haec belli summa nefandi.
> ferte faces propere foedusque reposcite flammis."

The Resolve to Fight

While leading the Trojans against the Greeks in the attack on the Achaean camp, Hector is described by the following simile (*Il.* XIII. 137–44):

> The Trojans came down on them in a pack, and Hektor
> led them
> raging straight forward, like a great rolling stone from a
> rock face
> that a river swollen with winter rain has wrenched from its
> socket
> and with immense washing broken the hold of the unwilling
> rock face;
> the springing boulder flies on, and the forest thunders
> beneath it;
> and the stone runs unwavering on a strong course, till it
> reaches
> the flat land, then rolls no longer for all its onrush;
> so Hector for awhile threatened. . . .[29]

Vergil adapts this simile to describe Turnus immediately after he learns that Aeneas, in his absence, has turned towards the city and is about to burn it to the ground; Amata, moreover, has just committed suicide. Vergil describes his emotions as follows (665–68):

> obstipuit varia confusus imagine rerum
> Turnus et obtutu tacito stetit; aestuat ingens
> uno in corde pudor mixtoque insania luctu
> et furiis agitatus amor et conscia virtus.

Aware of his shame, he resolves to face Aeneas, and as he turns from Juturna, he addresses her with an impassioned speech, which concludes (680–91):

> ". . . hunc oro, sine me furere ante furorem."
> dixit, et e curru saltum dedit ocius arvis
> perque hostis, per tela ruit maestamque sororem
> deserit ac rapido cursu media agmina rumpit.
> ac veluti montis saxum de vertice praeceps
> cum ruit avulsum vento, seu turbidus imber
> proluit aut annis solvit sublapsa vetustas;
> fertur in abruptum magno mons improbus actu
> exsultatque solo, silvas armenta virosque
> involvens secum: disiecta per agmina Turnus
> sic urbis ruit ad muros, ubi plurima fuso
> sanguine terra madet striduntque hastilibus aurae. . . .

It is clear that the Vergilian simile is modeled closely upon the one which Homer uses to describe Hector, and is still more appropriate in its context in the *Aeneid*.

Turnus's reaction to the news together with the simile is directly contrasted with the picture of Aeneas as he learns that his opponent will at long last come face to face with him (697–703):

> At pater Aeneas audito nomine Turni
> deserit et muros et summas deserit arces
> praecipitatque moras omnis, opera omnia rumpit
> laetitia exsultans horrendumque intonat armis:
> quantus Athos aut quantus Eryx aut ipse coruscis
> cum fremit ilicibus quantus gaudetque nivali
> vertice se attollens pater Appenninus ad auras.

This simile in turn was doubtlessly suggested by another in *Iliad* XIII again used to describe Hector, this time as he sets

out to reorganize the shaken Trojan forces in their renewed
assault on the Achaean camp (754–55):

> So he spoke, and went on his way like a snowy mountain,
> calling aloud, and swept through the Trojans and their com-
> panions.

The greater appropriateness of the Vergilian simile has
drawn the attention of Leaf[30] and Pöschl. Both spoke of the
two Vergilian similes in juxtaposition pointing to the marked
contrast between them and their symbolic significance:

> The boulder which hurtles down to the valley and leaves
> behind it a path of destruction and the majestic might
> and deep-rooted permanence of the eternally enduring moun-
> tain, the gloominess and brightness, the tumbling down
> and the "soaring into the sky," the sombre and brilliant
> tones—not only is the contrast between Turnus and Aeneas
> expressed in these opposing symbols but also between vic-
> tory and defeat, demonic and divine powers, barbaric and
> Roman ways, between the ephemeral force of wild destruc-
> tion and a might that endures all time. And this effect
> has grown in Vergil's hands out of Homer's three words,
> "like a snowy mountain," which convey only an optical
> impression.[31]

There is a striking similarity between Pöschl's appreciation
of these two Vergilian similes and the scholiasts' commentary on
the Homeric originals. As we have already noted (pp. 42 ff.),
the ancient scholars felt that Homer had used his simile of a
tumbling boulder to portray Hector's inner, emotional state in
addition to the violence of his attack. For them the rock rolling
wildly down the mountain slope was symbolic of Hector's
"barbaric irrationality." Needless to say, it might in all fairness
be objected that in no clearly evidenced way can Hector at
this point be described as "unstable."[32]

Vergil's adaptation of this simile, together with its symbolic
significance as understood by the ancient literary critics, in
describing the violence of Turnus's charge and the turbulence
of his emotional reactions to Saces' report is actually far more
appropriate: Vergil clearly wished to delineate Turnus's inherent
"barbaric irrationality"/"instability" by means of this carefully

adapted image, as his characterization of the Rutulian prince in the lines immediately preceding indicates. Turnus, on first learning of the assault on Laurentum, is described as having been struck by "varying emotions" (667 ff.). He immediately regained his senses, and after his impassioned speech to Juturna, again lapsed into a furious rage (680).[33]

The scholiasts' commentary on the second Homeric simile, in which Hector is likened to a snowcapped mountain, is equally worthy of note: to them it would appear that the snowy peak implied somewhat more than what Pöschl terms merely an "optical impression":

N 754: ὄρεϊ νιφόεντι) . . . πρὸς δὲ μέγεθος ἡ εἰκών, ἐπεὶ ἀκίνητόν ἐστι τὸ ὄρος. [BT] ἅμα δὲ καὶ τὸ ἄγριον αὐτοῦ καὶ φοβερὸν ὄρει παρεικάζει χιόνι κεκαλυμμένῳ · τὸ γὰρ ἄνιφον πάντως καὶ ἥμερον. [T]

Like a snowy mountain) . . . The simile is for size [greatness] since a mountain is immovable [steadfast]. [BT] At the same time he also compares his savage and terrifying [appearance] to a mountain which is covered with snow; for a mountain without snow is altogether the opposite [tame, cultivated, civilized]. [T]

So, too, did the simile suggest more to Vergil. Aeneas, likened to snow-peaked *pater Appenninus*, stands immutable and mighty (ἀκίνητον) in both his power and resolve, as opposed to the "ephemeral" and untamed, irresolute fury of Turnus as he rushes blindly toward his foe, compared to the rock bounding wildly down the mountain slope and involving all in its path in its own destruction.

The use of these two similes to describe the character and action of the two heroes becomes still more striking in their context in view of the earlier portrayal of Turnus's emotional reactions (*Aen.* XII. 101 ff., 220 ff., 614 ff., and so on), as opposed to Aeneas's steady resolve (107 ff., 311 ff., 466 ff., 697 ff., and so forth).[34] Indeed, the portrayal of Turnus's irrational and unstable emotions reaches its apex in this remarkable simile. Even as we may be certain that the juxtaposition and antithesis of these Homeric similes was no coincidence, so too, we may be

assured that Vergil was acutely aware of the deeper significance of the symbolic interpretations of the ancient scholars.
The greater effectiveness of the Vergilian similes lies precisely in
their juxtaposition and in the greater propriety of the context
for which they were adapted.

The Pursuit

The two heroes immediately clash. After a brief skirmish
Turnus's sword shatters and he turns to flee (742–45):

> ergo amens diversa fuga petit aequora Turnus
> et nunc huc, inde huc incertos implicat orbis;
> undique enim densa Teucri inclusere corona
> atque hinc vasta palus, hinc ardua moenia cingunt.

Aeneas, though hindered by his recent wound nevertheless
tenaciously pursues him (749–55):

> inclusum veluti si quando flumine nactus
> cervum aut puniceae saeptum formidine pennae
> venator cursu canis et latratibus instat;
> ille autem insidiis et ripa territus alta
> mille fugit refugitque vias, et vividus Umber
> haeret hians, iam iamque tenet similisque tenenti
> increpuit malis morsuque elusus inani est. . . .

This simile is an adaptation of one used in *Iliad* XXII to
describe Achilles' pursuit of Hector in the same situation (188–
93):

> But swift Achilles kept unremittingly after Hektor,
> chasing him, as a dog in the mountains who has flushed
>   from his covert
> a deer's fawn follows him through the folding ways and the
>   valleys,
> and though the fawn crouched down under a bush and be
>   hidden,
> he keeps running and noses him out until he comes on him;
> so Hektor could not lose himself from the fleet-footed
>   Peleion.

The scholiasts point out that while the simile is apt for the
pursuit in general, Hector, unlike the fawn, does not hide but
flees with the hope of gaining the safety of the walls. However,

as often as Hector turned toward the citadel, Achilles succeeded in turning him back toward the plain:

X 193: ὡς "Εκτωρ οὐ λῆθε) ἡ παραβολὴ πρὸς τὴν δίω-ξιν μόνον · οὐδὲ γὰρ κρύπτεται ὁ "Εκτωρ. ἢ ὅτι καὶ αὐτὸς καιρὸν παρεφύλαττε <τοῦ> ὑποφυγεῖν εἰς τὴν πόλιν, ὡς ὁ νεβρὸς εἰς τὸν θάμνον. [BT]

So Hektor could not lose himself) The simile is for [the concept of] the pursuit only, for Hector does not hide. Or because he watches closely for a chance to escape into the city, as the fawn does into the thicket.

Vergil has again taken a simile and varied it to suit the circumstance more closely; the stag does not hide but darts in countless directions in its efforts to escape the relentless hound. Like the stag, which is hemmed in by the hound, the bright snares, and the river and its high bank, so Turnus is hemmed in by Aeneas, the battlements of the city, and a marsh, in addition to the Trojans who are watching the struggle nearby. Vergil, in this instance, has taken the Homeric simile within its context and expanded it so that the comparison becomes more precise. All the elements are therefore represented by parallel componentsin the revised simile with the result that the objections raised by the scholiast, however insignificant they might be, have been removed.

After another simile, which describes the futility of the chase, Homer next provides an answer to the question which naturally arises from the situation, for he tells us why the Achaeans do not rush to Achilles' aid while he struggles in vain to catch the fleeing Hector (205–7):

But brilliant Achilleus kept shaking his head at his own people
and would not let them throw their bitter projectiles at Hektor
for fear the thrower might win the glory, and himself come second.

Megacleides, in characteristic fashion, ridiculed the prodigious nod:

X 205: λαοῖσι δ᾽ ἀνένευε) Μεγακλείδης πλάσμα εἶναί
φησι τοῦτο τὸ μονομάχιον · [BT] πῶς γὰρ τοσαύτας μυ-
ριάδας νεύματι ᾽Αχιλλεὺς ἀπέστρεφεν; [B]³⁵

Kept shaking his head at his own people) Megacleides says
that this single combat is unrealistically constructed, for
how could Achilles restrain so many myriads [of warriors]?

Vergil has also imitated this incident, but has turned it
about in his own characteristic way. When the two warriors first
draw near one another, Vergil tells us that all the forces on both
sides laid down their arms and sought the best vantage point
for viewing the combat; they are under a truce. When Turnus
is forced to flee weaponless, he beseeches the Rutulians to bring
him his own sword (758–62):

ille simul fugiens Rutulos simul increpat omnis
nomine quemque vocans notumque efflagitat ensem.
Aeneas mortem contra praesensque minatur
exitium, si quisquam adeat, terretque trementis
excisurum urbem minitans et saucius instat.

Regardless of what one might think of Megacleides' criticism as
preserved in the scholia, it must be admitted that Achilles' nod
puts a slight strain on belief. However, in keeping with his
characterization of Achilles, Homer has his hero, who is concerned with his own honor and glory, warn his allies not to
come to his aid: Hector will be his prey, and his alone. Aeneas's
threat to any of his enemies who might be minded to come to
Turnus's aid is by contrast a logical result of the situation as it
stands. The Rutulians would naturally be anxious for their
champion and willing and eager to help him were it not for the
presence of the Trojans and the dire threat of Aeneas. And as
if to make the incident all the more credible, Vergil has added
that the Rutulians were already terrified (761).

Divine Intervention

In order to bring the combat between Hector and Achilles to
a decisive issue, Athena, with the approval of Zeus, takes on the
guise of Deiphobus, one of Hector's brothers, and addresses the
Trojan hero assuring him that she will stand by his side if he

will face his adversary.[36] The objection of the scholiast to such a deceit on the part of a deity is brief:

X 227: Δηϊφόβῳ εἰκυῖα) ἄτοπον θεὸν οὖσαν πλανᾶν τὸν
Ἕκτορα. ἢ τὰ ἴσα πράττει Ἀπόλλωνι, ἐπεὶ κἀκεῖνος
ἐπέθετο Πατρόκλῳ καὶ Ἀχιλλεῖ. [B] . . . ἐπέθετο Πατρόκλῳ μαχομένῳ [*Il.* XVI. 793]. [T]

Likened herself to Deiphobus) It is unfitting for the goddess to deceive Hector. Or, she does the same thing as Apollo when he set upon Patroclus and Achilles. [B] . . . set upon Patroclus in battle. [T]

This incident is handled quite differently in the *Aeneid*, though a deity does intervene on behalf of her favorite. As Heinze has already pointed out, Juno had instigated deception during the course of the action even before the duel, but this was to preserve the life of Turnus.[37] Juturna, in the disguise of Metiscus, had kept Turnus away from Aeneas for his own preservation, and had instigated the breaking of the truce for the same reason. Still disguised as Metiscus, Juturna gave Turnus back his sword while Faunus, in answer to his prayer, held Aeneas's spear fast as it stuck in the ancient tree stump. Then, and only then, did Venus intervene on behalf of Aeneas by wrenching the spear loose. Achilles succeeds with the aid of the goddess who deceives his foe; in the *Aeneid*, the hero fights without any divine aid until his antagonist is given an unnatural advantage by the deities who favor him.[38]

The intervention of Athena during the climactic duel of the *Iliad* is by no means the only occasion in which Homer causes the gods to act deceitfully; both of the aforementioned scholia refer back to the death of Patroclus, which is brought about by a still more underhanded act of the gods. When Patroclus is on the verge of scaling the walls of Troy, he is thrust back by a dire warning from Apollo who then rouses Hector to enter the battle (*Il.* XVI. 698 ff.), acts in themselves not subject to censure. After Patroclus kills Cebriones and the Achaeans succeed in capturing his body from the Trojans, Patroclus rushes into the midst of the enemy three times slaying nine men. At this point Homer addresses him (786–93):

but as for the fourth time he swept in, like something greater
than human, there, Patroclus, the end of your life was
shown forth,
since Phoibos came against you there in the strong encounter
dangerously, nor did Patroclus see him as he moved through
the battle, and shrouded in a deep mist came in against him
and stood behind him, and struck his back and his broad
shoulders
with a flat stroke of the hand so that his eyes spun. Phoibos
Apollo now struck away from his head the helmet. . . .

His spear then shattered, and the baldric fell from his shoulders,
while Apollo loosened his corslet. Euphorbus immediately struck
the dazed Patroclus in the back with his spear. As Patroclus
slowly retreated unarmed, Hector dealt him his death blow.

The scholiasts comment first on the rather curious partiality which Homer shows here and elsewhere toward Patroclus,
which at this point detracts from Hector's *aristeia*:[39]

Π 793: κρατὸς κυνέην βάλε) ἐντεῦθεν ἔστιν ὁρᾶν τὴν προσ-
πάθειαν τοῦ ποιητοῦ, ὅτι τὴν ἀριστείαν τοῦ "Εκτορος
τῷ 'Απόλλωνι περιτίθησιν. [A]

Struck the helmet from his head) Here one can see the
poet's passionate attachment in that he puts Hector's *aristeia* into Apollo's hands.

Such partiality is totally absent from *Aeneid* XII, as is Athena's
deceitful intervention, which if nothing else, as the scholiasts
realized, detracts from the dramatic effect of the action. Indeed,
we may say that precisely the opposite is the case. Far from
being deceived by a deity in this climactic scene of the *Aeneid*,
Turnus is manifestly condemned by the *Dira* which Jupiter has
sent to drive Juturna from the field (843–86). His terror is
complete (865–68):

hanc versa in faciem Turni se pestis ob ora
fertque refertque sonans clipeumque everberat alis.
illi membra novus solvit formidine torpor,
arrectaeque horrore comae et vox faucibus haesit.

He now realizes that it is the will of Jupiter himself that de-
stroys him and, as his reply to Aeneas's taunt would indicate,

that his abandonment by the powers of universal order and justice is total (894–95):

"... non me tua fervida terrent
dicta, ferox; di me terrent et Iuppiter hostis."[40]

Again, the opening words of Turnus's last speech in the *Aeneid*, words which also are not to found in Hector's dying plea, reveal the full awareness of his own guilt (931–32):

"equidem merui nec deprecor," inquit;
"utere sorte tua. . . ."

Herein, perhaps, lies the crucial difference in concept and meaning between the deaths of Hector and Turnus.

Nightmare and Abandonment

The fear and futility of Turnus's last actions are vividly described by a simile modeled in concept on one which also describes the futility toward the end of the combat between Hector and Achilles. In the *Iliad*, however, the simile expresses the futility which both warriors feel as Hector is unable to escape Achilles, nor is Achilles able to overtake Hector in the chase (XXII. 199–201):

> As in a dream a man is not able to follow one who runs
> from him, nor can the runner escape, nor the other pursue him,
> so he could not run him down in his speed, nor the other
> get clear.

The simile was athetized presumably by Aristarchus on the grounds that it was weak in expression as well as in its effect; moreover, it does not seem to suit the situation insofar as it does not take into account Achilles' swiftness of foot:

X 199: ὡς δ' ἐν ὀνείρῳ) ἀθετοῦνται στίχοι τρεῖς, ὅτι καὶ
τῇ κατασκευῇ καὶ τῷ νοήματι εὐτελεῖς · καὶ γὰρ ἀπραξίαν
δρόμου καὶ τὸ ἀπαράβατον σημαίνουσιν, ἐναντίως τῷ
"ὡς δέ τ' ἀεθλοφόροι περὶ τέρματα μώνυχες ἵπποι"
[162]. [A]
τὸ ἄπρακτον θέλοι δηλῶσαι · ὡς γὰρ ἐκεῖνοι φαντασίᾳ
καὶ οὐκ ἀληθείᾳ εἰσίν, οὕτω καὶ οὗτοι οὐδὲν ἤνυον, οὔτε
οὗτός τὸ φεύγειν οὔτε οὗτος τὸ καταλαβεῖν . . . . [BT]
ἄλλως: ἀθετοῦνται οἵ γ' διὰ τὸ ἀσθενὲς τῆς φράσεως καὶ
ὅτι ὑπεκλύουσι τὴν ποδώκειαν Ἀχιλλέως. [T][41]

As in a dream) These three lines are athetized because they
are weak ["shabby"] in construction and thought, for they
show both the futility of the chase and the lack of motion
[lit., inalterability] contrary to the idea of [the race horse
simile] "As when about the turnposts racing single-footed
horses . . ." (XXII. 162). [A]
He would like to show their lack of success, for just as
those [in the dream] are in a state of seeming, and not in
reality, so these two could accomplish nothing, neither in
flight nor in capture. . . . [BT] Otherwise: these three lines
are athetized because of their weakness in expression and
because they ignore ["weaken the force of"] Achilles' swiftness
of foot. [T]

Aristarchus (?) has been criticized in recent times for his objections to this simile, and it would seem that scholium T preserves
a rejection of the athetesis in keeping with contemporary taste.
The simile, if nothing else, is a striking one, and well-suited as
an expression of the frustration and futility both warriors
would feel, as though both were experiencing a nightmare or
some fantastic flight of the imagination.

Vergil has so varied the action of the pursuit of Turnus
that he was able to adapt the germ of this magnificent simile
and use it all the more effectively and in his own way, still
more appropriately than Homer. There is no question of
Turnus's ability to outdistance Aeneas, whose wound, Vergil
has reminded us, had slowed him down (746 f.). The simile of
the race horses (*Il.* XXII. 162 ff.) has been omitted, perhaps
to remove the objection that the dream simile was not in keeping
with its effect, and in its place Vergil has substituted the simile
of the Umbrian hound (749–55).

After Juturna's intervention and that of Venus to counter-
balance it, and the subsequent discussion between Juno and
Jupiter, Jupiter sends the demon to drive Juturna from the
field. Aeneas then warns Turnus that he cannot escape. Turnus,
with a brief reply, picks up a huge rock (901–14):[42]

ille manu raptum trepida torquebat in hostem
altior insurgens et cursu concitus heros.
. sed neque currentem se nec cognoscit euntem
tollentemve manus saxumve immane moventem;

genua labant, gelidus concrevit frigore sanguis.
tum lapis ipse viri vacuum per inane volutus
nec spatium evasit totum neque pertulit ictum.
ac velut in somnis, oculos ubi languida pressit
nocte quies, nequiquam avidos extendere cursus
velle videmur et in mediis conatibus aegri
succidimus—non lingua valet, non corpore notae
sufficiunt vires nec vox aut verba sequuntur:
sic Turno, quacumque viam virtute petivit,
successum dea dira negat. . . .

In this virtually surrealistic fashion Vergil has appropriated
the "dream simile" to portray Turnus's terror and anxiety. The
simile has little in common with the original except for this
terrible sensation of futility and helplessness that we experience
in dreams, nor does it apply, as it does in the *Iliad*, to both
combatants. It is concerned only with the one who now at
last knows that his fate is upon him and that the gods themselves are against him, as indeed Turnus realizes.[43] This, for
all its pathos, is the crux of this last simile, as it is of the con-
cluding scene of the *Aeneid*.[44]

VII

Summary and Conclusion

The poets of the late Republican and Augustan period were heirs of the great mass of Hellenistic literary creativity and scholarship.[1] Although the predominant interest of these Greek scholars might loosely be termed "literary propriety," it should be reemphasized that this was an all-encompassing principle which included not merely comment on social and religious mores but, of more importance, criticism of the appropriateness of characterization, motivation of action, unity, plot, and effectiveness of poetic image. Allegorical interpretations were also part of Homeric criticism, especially at Pergamum and in the Stoic schools. Of most importance, perhaps, is the fact that in the hands of these Hellenistic scholars, various Homeric figures and incidents had become exemplars of right or wrong action and certain similes and images had taken on specific symbolic meanings. Every educated reader in antiquity was well trained in these moral criticisms and aesthetic appreciations of the *Iliad* and the *Odyssey*, if only as a result of the standard schooling of the times.

The Hellenistic criticism of the Homeric poems was as well known to Roman students of Homer as the leading commentaries of a major author are to scholars today, and the ancient text and commentary were regarded as a unit, as integral parts of a single literary tradition. It is unquestionably within this framework of traditional interpretation that Vergil began to formulate the basis for his reinterpretation of the Homeric poems, their meaning for his own generation, and the new order of things that he envisioned. The *Aeneid*, no mere translation of the *Iliad* or *Odyssey*, is indeed a mosaic of passages from these epics which Vergil carefully chose, adapted, and artistically integrated into his own work in his effort to create an epic worthy to rank with those of Homer.

Once again, it is necessary to stress that this is not to imply that Vergil, who obviously had his own convictions in matters of literary criticism, would have felt himself constrained in any way to abide by the *dicta* of the Hellenistic scholars. However, Vergil was not writing in a literary vacuum. The mere fact that he deliberately chose to incorporate his own variations on so many Homeric lines and episodes that had been criticized by these scholars is in itself sufficient grounds for believing that Vergil was sensitive to the traditional observations and eager to exploit the associations already in the minds of his readers. Such exploitation of traditional Homeric episodes and their interpretations would most effectively serve to heighten the contrast between the old and the new vision of epic that Vergil surely intended.

The vast majority of the scholia discussed throughout this study are on those passages which Vergil appropriated in the course of his composition of *Aeneid* I., IX., and XII. This is understandable since these three books are consistently the most "Homeric" of the entire *Aeneid*, and it is in them that we should most expect to discover evidence of Vergil's attempts to compete with Homer.

Although some of the scholia may seem to bear only a coincidental resemblance to a given passage in the *Aeneid*, the recurrence of several or more within an episode would lend greater support to the view that Vergil was influenced by Homeric criticism. It is hoped, therefore, that the cumulative effect of the number and variety of the examples cited especially within the episodes of these three books will have sufficed to preclude the possibility that similarities between Vergil's *retractatio* and the scholiasts' commentaries are simply coincidental. The following summary briefly examines the use Vergil appears to have made of the traditional criticisms and interpretations of the Homeric poems.

Glosses

The most obvious benefit of Homeric scholarship, certainly for Roman readers, was the glosses and discussions of archaic and obscure words. To what extent we may safely and objectively say that a specific gloss influenced Vergil's interpretation of a word or words must remain a moot point, yet we have seen on occasion that Vergil appears to have expanded a specific interpretation of a word in question in the light of the scholiasts' remarks rather than to have simply employed a Latin synonym to render a literal translation (pp. 20 ff.). In such instances we are dealing with interpretations of meaning not for an isolated word so much as with an interpretation of poetic intent within a still larger framework of meaning. This is clear, for example, in the scholia on the Paris-stallion simile (pp. 26 ff.). Homer employed the simile to portray Paris's spirited confidence and speed as he proudly strode forth through the citadel in quest of Hector so that they might both renew the battle with the Achaeans. The scholiasts questioned the meaning of ἀκοστήσας, *a hapax legomenon*, and suggested that it would be better taken to mean "restive because of his inactivity at the manger" (A on Z 506) rather than "full-fed" (Ennius's *fartus*). κροαίνειν (gallop) was likewise taken metaphorically to mean "yearn," at least by the *neôteroi* and Archilochus (Aristarchus?). The mane, moreover, was seen as the source of the stallion's pride and befitting Paris's handsome appearance. In short the scholiasts were attempting by their interpretations of both words to understand the simile not so much as a simple visual comparison but rather as a unified psychological analogy: καὶ τὸ παράδειγμα ἀπὸ γαυρικοῦ ἵππου καὶ ἀλογίστου. [B] The point of comparison is [taken] from a haughty [arrogant] and irrational horse.

This, of course, is precisely the point of Vergil's adaptation and expansion of this simile to describe Turnus as he exuberantly bursts forth from the confines of the assembly and eagerly strides on to marshal his troops for battle. We may reasonably conclude that Vergil considered the exegesis of these words and that his final execution of the simile was colored by the tradition opposed to the one which Ennius had chosen to accept.

Symbolic Interpretation

Examination of exegesis on Homeric imagery in general readily reveals the Hellenistic scholars' preoccupation with symbolic interpretations and their efforts to see the similes as extending beyond the outer, visual description of an action to an inner, psychological characterization of the figure involved. Closely akin to allegorical interpretations, these imaginative appreciations were doubtlessly well known, if not to casual readers of Homer, then certainly to scholars of literature. For the scholiasts the snake coiling around the plane tree in *Iliad* II had become a symbolic prophecy of the devious and treacherous means of the Achaeans' ultimate sack of Troy (pp. 37 ff.). In Vergil's hands this omen as interpreted in the scholia, recurs not so much as the serpents that devour Laocoon and his sons but as the dominant image of the entire *Iliu Persis* of *Aeneid* II. Vergil's choice, likewise, of critical events from the future history of Rome as the device for Aeneas's shield was surely occasioned by the various interpretations of Achilles' shield as a symbol of democracy or of the early history of Athens (pp. 33 ff.). Symbolic interpretations of lion similes in the *Iliad* may well lie behind Vergil's use of similar comparisons throughout the latter half of the *Aeneid* to serve, in effect, as his commentary on the action (pp. 44 ff.). In this respect, one of the more significant examples is the simile which likens Turnus to a rock rolling wildly down a mountain slope (pp. 95 ff.). The same simile in the *Iliad* had been interpreted as symbolic of Hector's "barbaric irrationality" as he rushed furiously against the Achaean fortifications. Here, too, when a related metaphor was used of Hector in an earlier book, Porphyry's reference to what we may term "continuity of imagery" shows clearly that the ancient reader also looked for a deeper and more extended meaning in Homeric imagery (pp. 41 ff.). We may readily assume, therefore, that Vergil also expected his readers to re-

cognize the significance of his use of Homeric imagery, especially when based upon the traditional literary criticism that
had grown up around the *Iliad* and the *Odyssey*.

Realism: Nisus and Euryalus

Brooks Otis has termed the Nisus-Euryalus episode "essentially paradigmatic" and, comparing it with the *Dolonia*, states
that "the difference between Virgil's *exemplary* (Otis's italics)
and Homer's merely *narrative* intention is quite apparent."[2]
The scholiasts, however, despite their frequent criticisms of
Homer's narrative technique throughout the episode, did see
somewhat more than a "merely narrative intention" in the
Dolonia. Diomedes' decision to volunteer for the dangerous
mission was sharply contrasted with Hector's offer of pay and
Dolon's demand for further reward (pp. 63 ff.). In this respect
Vergil seems to have made an even greater contrast in portraying Nisus's decision to undertake the mission as purely
voluntary with no need for a request from a commanding
officer, and hence, truly magnanimous and heroic (pp. 66 ff.).
The scholiasts, though they comment at length on the prudent
choice of inconspicuous armor for the venture (pp. 69 ff.), on
the other hand, criticized Homer's want of realistic motivation
for the action because of the lateness of the hour and the apparent failure of the Greek pair to attempt to accomplish their
mission in their eagerness for spoils (pp. 75 ff.). Again Vergil's
narrative technique contrasts sharply with Homer's. Because
of the lateness of the hour and because of their eagerness for
spoils, the Trojan pair do not accomplish their mission but
rather perish, betrayed just before dawn by the light of the
moon glancing from the decoration of Euryalus's plundered helmet (pp. 72 ff.).

Motivation

Perhaps the most elementary and certainly basic type of Homeric
criticism concerns the motivation and unity of action. Where

Homeric motivation is clearly found wanting, one might readily assume that Vergil was more than competent to have been his own critic. On several occasions, however, we have noted that Vergil appears to have incorporated the gist of the scholiasts' suggestions as to "improvement" into his own redevelopment of the action of the *Iliad*. Here especially, a comparison of the two poets and the ancient criticism establishes a touchstone for our understanding of Vergil's new interpretation of heroism and its meaning. In his appropriation of the "Breaking of the Truce," for example, Vergil's main points of departure stem from the passages criticized in the scholia, and in keeping with the spirit of their comments, he has developed the action so as to emphasize his characterization of the figures involved (pp. 85 ff.). In particular, Aeneas's dedication to the oath of the armistice is stressed and maintained despite the treacherous attack on the Trojans, and consequently, upon himself. This surely, in contrast with Hector and hence Turnus, is the real purpose behind Vergil's adaptation of this episode.

Characterization

Equally important is Vergil's characterization of Aeneas at the very opening of his epic, in a situation taken directly from the *Odyssey*. Odysseus, purporting to encourage his men with plans and hopes for the future, concludes by telling them in effect that he can see no escape from their predicament. Aristarchus felt that Homer intended these words as Odysseus's thought to himself, and accordingly had placed them in parenthesis (pp. 53 ff.). This is precisely how Vergil developed Aeneas's speech, given alike on the shores of a forlorn and unknown land. At its conclusion, Vergil adds (I. 208–9):

> Talia voce refert curisque ingentibus aeger
> spem vultu simulat, premit altum corde dolorem.

Here, at the critical moment, Vergil is relying upon his readers' recognition of his departure from his model. He has, in short, served notice that his concept of hero will depart dramatically from that of the Greek epic.

Propriety and the Gods

Adverse criticisms of Homer on the grounds of social or religious impropriety are naturally of little consequence in view of the seven centuries (ca.) and two different cultures which separate Vergil and Homer. Still, since Vergil chose openly to imitate well-known passages which had been censured on just these grounds, we may be certain that he was aware of the traditional criticisms and that his adaptations of Homer were not simply to display to his audience a mere technical superiority in the *agôn*. On the contrary, we may assume that his purpose was of singular importance, as indeed is his portrayal of Latinus's offer of Lavinia's hand in marriage to Aeneas at the very opening of the second half of the *Aeneid* (pp. 10 ff.). Here, quite in contrast to Alcinous's offer of his daughter to the stranger Odysseus, in a passage that would leap to the mind of every discerning reader of the *Aeneid*, this marriage had at some point before Aeneas's arrival been openly ordained by the gods. Despite the oracles and portents, however, Turnus's jealousy and frustration over the proposal serve as the basis for the six books of warfare that conclude the *Aeneid*, as Turnus's final words at Aeneas's sword point also reveal (XII. 937 f.):

> ". . . tua est Lavinia coniunx,
> ulterius ne tende odiis."

In spite of Turnus's destructive rage, Latinus's indecisions, and the Latins' willingness to fight on behalf of their champion, Vergil has made it quite clear in his adaptation of the Alcinous-Odysseus passage that it is by divine sanction and decree that Aeneas shall marry Lavinia: there can be no charge of impropriety in this offer of a maiden's hand to a foreigner and stranger.

Toward the close of the duel between Hector and Achilles, Athena deceitfully lures the Trojan hero to his death in a passage also censured by the ancient scholars on the grounds of its impropriety (pp. 101 ff.). Though the gods in both epics are equally intent on the outcome, and the fate of each hero has been placed in the balance, there is no such deceit that leads to Turnus's death. On the contrary, Jupiter openly manifests his doom by the *Dira* sent to drive Juturna from the field. Unlike Hector, who becomes aware of Athena's deception and realizes that his death is at hand, Turnus is terrified and collapses with the realization of his own guilt and the total abandonment by the powers of divine justice and order.

The Agôn

Vergil's appropriation of Homeric imagery served to maintain the illusion of traditional epic as well as to add a deeper dimension to his own poetry. By developing and systematizing the symbolic significance which the Hellenistic scholars had seen as latent or expressed throughout the *Iliad*, Vergil was able to transfigure the haunting qualities of Homeric imagery not only for its own sake as poetic adornment but more importantly for his own interpretative analysis of the action and characterization in the *Aeneid*.[3] The function, effectiveness, and originality of Vergil's use of Homeric imagery become clearer when viewed in the light of the Hellenistic interpretations out of which it was surely developed.

One question remains: granted that Vergil chose to use the legendary foundation of Rome by Trojan refugees, which had been and must be set against a Homeric background, how might he most effectively set off in high relief his new interpretation of epic and hero? In other words, why should Vergil appropriate passages thought to have been defective by the most eminent scholars of antiquity if it were not for the fact, as many have felt, that the Roman poet wished to challenge Homer on his own grounds, and indeed, to reject him?[4] The theory of the *agôn* is valid and helps to explain some of the many tantalizing differences of plot, characterization, and even tone between the Vergilian and Homeric epics in those areas where they are externally most similar. In each of the criticized passages cited immediately above, Vergil has chosen not simply to vary but to reverse the ultimate outcome of the

Homeric episode: (1) Nisus and Euryalus do not return to their camp laden with spoils as did Diomedes and Odysseus; they die for their failure to accomplish their mission. (2) Aeneas, in direct contrast to Hector or Turnus, does struggle heroically to prevent the Trojans from breaking the truce. (3) Aeneas's words of encouragement and promise of safety to his men, despite his suppressed despair, will be fulfilled and the Trojans will reach their promised land, all of which is quite in contrast to the *Odyssey*.[5] (4) Aeneas, unlike Odysseus, is well known by prophecy to Latinus and will marry Lavinia. (5) Turnus, far from being deceived by a divinity, is manifestly condemned by Jupiter, an act which he realizes not only means his death but his guilt in the eyes of men and gods.

It is precisely in his adaptation of these passages of alleged "weakness" that Vergil has often portrayed most pointedly his vision of epic hero and meaning, of Rome and destiny. Openly contrasting crucial scenes of his epic with their Homeric proto-types, he has frequently exploited the traditional literary scholarship as a means of helping to crystallize his concept of epic for his own contemporary audience. It is in this respect that the scholiasts' interpretations provide an additional dimen-sion to comparison of Homer and Vergil—a comparison original-ly demanded by the Roman poet, and one whose meaning becomes richer with a knowledge of Hellenistic criticism and exegesis.

Abbreviations

AJP	*American Journal of Philology*
CJ	*Classical Journal*
CR	*Classical Review*
GRBS	*Greek Roman and Byzantine Studies*
JRS	*Journal of Roman Studies*
LEC	*Les Études Classiques*
LSJ	*A Greek English Lexicon by H. Liddell and R. Scott,* a New Edition, rev. by H. S. Jones and R. McKenzie (Oxford, 1940)
RE	Pauly-Wissowa, *Real-Encyclopädie der classischen Altertumswissenschaft*
TAPA	*Transactions of the American Philological Association*

Notes

Chapter I.

1. *Vita Verg.* 23–46; Quint. X. 3, 8; cf. Macrobius *Sat.* I. 24, 10–12, and Pliny *N. H.* XIV. 1, 7.

2. For Vergil as a rival of Homer, see Conington-Nettleship, *P. Vergili Maronis Opera* (3rd ed., London, 1883), II, pp. xxiv, xxxi, xxxviii, for an evaluation which is still useful; cf. also K. Büchner, *P. Vergilius Maro: der Dichter der Römer* (Stuttgart, 1956), p. 246, and G. Knauer, "Vergil's *Aeneid* and Homer," *GRBS* V (1964), p. 64. For discussions of this *agôn* or *retractio*, see A.-M. Guillemin, *L'originalité de Virgile* (Paris, 1932), pp. 125–33, and especially A. Severyns, "Virgile et Homère," *Il Mondo Classico*, I (1931), pp. 42–55, where the term *surenchère*, or the "outbidding" of one's opponent, is used of Vergil's approach to his "competition" with Homer.

3. It was expected that such literary borrowings would be recognized, as Seneca *Rhetor* intimates in his discussion of Ovid's appropriation of Vergil's lines (*Suas.* III. 7):

> fecisse, quod in multis aliis versibus Vergilii fecerat, non surripiendi causa sed palam mutuandi, hoc animo ut vellet agnosci.

Cf. also Ps.-Longinus *de Subl.* XIII. 4. The matter has recently been succinctly summarized by W. S. Anderson, "On Vergil's Use of the *Odyssey*," *Vergilius* 9 (1963), p. 1. Such an exploitation of associations already in the mind of the reader would naturally help to recreate the atmosphere, or illusion, of epic as it exists in reality, as it were, in the Homeric poems. Cf. also *Buc.* VIII. 69 and *Aen.* VI. 846.

4. Cf. B. Otis, *Virgil: A Study in Civilized Poetry* (Oxford, 1963), `p. 36.

5. See H. Fränkel, "Griechische Bildung in altrömischen Epen," *Hermes* 67 (1932), pp. 303–11 for a discussion of the use of Homeric glosses still extant in the scholia by Livius Andronicus in his translation of the *Odyssey*.

6. *de Ling. Lat.* VIII, 68 ff.; IX. 43.

7. Cf. also *ad Fam.* III. 11, 5; IX. 10, 1.

8. M. Van der Valk, *Researches on the Text and Scholia of the Iliad* (Leiden, 1964), pt. II, p. 148. See also W. Leaf, *The Iliad* (2nd ed., London, 1900), 1, p. 73, n. 318.

9. J. Tolkiehn, *Homer und die römische Poesie* (Leipzig, 1900), p. 47, n. 1.

10. For a study and discussion of Homeric criticism in antiquity, see R. Pfeiffer, *History of Classical Scholarship* (Oxford, 1968) especially pt. II, "The Hellenistic Age." See also Christ, Schmid, Stählin, *Geschichte der griechische Litteratur*, I, pp. 78–87 and II, pp. 259 ff.; M. Van der Valk, *op. cit.*, I, pp. 536 ff.

11. For the discussion, see *Mitteilungen aus der Papyrussammlung der Oesterreichischen Nationalbibliothek*, N. S., V (1956), p. 54 and n. 2.

12. *de Gram.*, 2. This remark, however, tells us little. See also A. J. Podlecki, "The Peripatetics as Literary Critics," *Phoenix* XXIII (1969), pp. 114–42, especially pp. 116–17.

13. See his review of the "Harvard Servius," *JRS* 39 (1949), pp. 145–54. See also M. Mühmelt, *Griechische Grammatik in der Vergilerklärung*, Zetemata 37 (1965).

14. See pp. 15, 17; see also pp. 10 f., 54, 87, 89, 90 f.

Chapter II.

1. See his index under *Homerscholien*, *op. cit.*, p. 496 for a complete list. See note 3 below.

2. Cf. also schol. ET on ς 244, Nausicaa's wish that she be granted a husband like the stranger before her, lines also censured on the ground that the notion was ἀπρεπής. Alcinous, however, realized that the stranger wished to get

home, as indeed he says in the lines that follow. One might note that this observation seems to show that the scholiasts occasionally did consider differences of time and *mores* in their commentaries, and so exhibit some sense of "historical perspective."

3. Note also the reference to the ancient *mos*, which repeats the view suggested in scholium η 311. Of Latinus's address, and especially of his use of the name, *Dardanidae*, Heinze wrote: "Virgil will dem König die Ankömmlinge nicht völlig fremd sein lassen (er kennt auch v. 205 die italische Abstammung des Dardanos), um sein rasches Entgegenkommen namentlich mit dem Angebot der Ehe einigermassen vorzubereiten. Aristarch hatte es sehr unpassend gefunden, dass Alkinoos dem Odysseus, ohne ihn näher zu kennen, seine Tochter zur Ehe anbot: schol. η 311," *op. cit.*, p. 338, n. 1.

4. Cf. Mühmelt, *op. cit.*, on the relationship in general. For an interesting discussion of the Nausicaa scene in the *Odyssey* and the abundance of ancient criticism thereon, see E. E. Sikes, *The Greek View of Poetry* (London, 1931), pp. 163–68. See also M. Van der Valk, *Textual Criticism of the Odyssey* (Leiden, 1949), pp. 188 and 206.

5. W. Leaf, *The Iliad* (2nd ed., London, 1900), I, p. 6, n. 29–31, provides a good example.

6. See also schol. A on *Π* 668 οὕτως Ἀρίσταρχος, Σαρπηδόνι, κατὰ δοτικὴν . . .μήποτε [in the sense, "perhaps"] δὲ Ζηνόδοτος ὀρθῶς ἠθέτηκε τούτους. παράλογον γὰρ τὸν ἀπενθῆ τοιαῦτα διακονεῖσθαι. For further discussion of these lines, see Leaf, *op. cit.*, II, pp. 202 f., n. 666.

7. It should be noted that Vergil begins the *aristeia* of Camilla with a translation of the opening lines of Patroclus's *aristeia*: "quem telo primum, quem postremum, aspera virgo, deicis?" (664) *Il.* XVI. 692: "ἔνθα τίνα πρῶτον, τίνα δ' ὕστατον ἐξενάριξας, Πατρόκλεις . . .''; cf. *Il.* V. 703, where the same line is used of Hector, but in the third person, without the apostrophe.

8. See schol. A on *Π* 666, and Leaf, *loc. cit.*

9. For a discussion of the Camilla episode, see Heinze, *op. cit.*, pp. 227 ff. Vergil has successfully compressed the episode into a whole, unified by the presence of Opis, whereas Homer moves from Zeus to Hera to Apollo.

10. Sarpedon has his relatives, whereas the pathos is heightened in the case of Camilla, who is alone and without anyone to mourn her, save for Diana.

11. See pp. 102 ff., above, for further instances of "impropriety" in the deaths of Patroclus and Hector.

12. See R. D. Williams, *P. Vergili Maronis Aeneidos Liber V* (Oxford, 1960), p. xiv, and M. Putnam, *The Poetry of the Aeneid* (Cambridge, Mass., 1965), pp. 64 ff.

13. Heinze, *op. cit.*, p. 164.

14. Meriones (872–73) vows a sacrifice to Apollo as he shoots.

15. See e.g., schol. T. on Ψ 581 and Y 40.

16. Review of E. K. Rand, *et al.*, "The Harvard Servius," vol. II, in *JRS* 39 (1949), pp. 145–54, especially pp. 151 ff.

17. Minerva is referred to as Pallas in I. 479 in reference to her temple, the Palladium, and again in II. 166 and 183 as the image. In II. 163 Pallas is used as the goddess in whom the Greeks placed their hopes for success in war. In II. 15, Pallas is used for the name of the inspirer of the creation of the horse; only here is the name used without the same appropriate application as in the other instances. But cf. Servius, *ad loc.*: Palladis arte: aut 'ingeniose' aut 'dolose', ac si diceret 'consilio iratae deae', quae fuit inimica Troianis.

18. Cf. *Etym. Mag.* 767, 48 ff., which preserves a similar etymology. Though the "true" etymology of the word would appear to be closer to *tritôn* (*mer*), as some of the ancient scholars believed, this need not concern us here in view of the traditional meaning as preserved by Servius and the scholia.

19. I have omitted all references to the goddess as Minerva on the grounds that her name, as opposed to the variants, is neutral in meaning or is associated with her as the patroness of crafts. Cf. II. 31, 189, 404; III. 531; V. 284; VI. 840; VII. 805; VIII. 409, 699; XI. 259. In II. 615, the goddess is called both Tritonia and Pallas as she appears wreaking destruction on Troy as it blazes before the very eyes of Aeneas. Although the other references to her as Pallas and/or Tritonia are made in passing and are not concerned with her as an active agent in the plot, still, the variants seem to be significant in III. 544, VIII. 435, and XI. 483. Pallas is used in reference to the Palladium in IX. 151 and XI. 477.

In the only other references to the goddess in the *Aeneid*, Pallas in VII. 154 is used of the olive leaf and seems to bear no special significance; in V. 704, Tritonia Pallas is used in reference to the prophecy of fate or of the anger of the gods.

20. It is quite possible that in several of the examples cited above Vergil might well have relied on his *Schulwissen* for his interpretations of the Greek. This would be especially so in instances where he appears to have translated glosses or used epithets with careful attention to their traditional etymologies. Cf. Mühmelt's remarks on Servius's knowledge of the Homeric scholia, *op. cit.*, pp. 27, 48. Still, it would not be misleading to term such coincidence as examples of of an "indirect" influence of Hellenistic scholarship on the composition of the *Aeneid*.

21. See p. 118, n. 5, above, for Fränkel's article on the influence of the scholiastic tradition on Livius Andronicus.

22. "Vergil as a Student of Homer," *Martin Classical Lectures*, I (1930), pp. 151–81.

23. The word(s) or possibly the sign preceding the lemma does not appear in the mss. In the lines preceding Achilles' boast Homer does, however, tell us who the warrior was.

24. Cf. *Il.* II. 119–28 and Aristarchus's athetesis of l. 124 with *Aeneid* XII. 227–43, where Juturna repeats the substance of Agamemnon's words. Here, there is no unnecessary "supposition of details" in a hypothesis; indeed, it is the details that make the hypothesis cogent for her argument. See Leaf, *op. cit.*, I, p. 57, n. 124, who approves of the athetesis.

25. See Pierron, *op. cit.*, I, p. 204, n. 438, and Leaf, *op. cit.*, I, p. 250, n. 838–39. See also Bachmann, *op. cit.*, I, p. 29.

26. Conington-Nettleship, *op. cit.*, II, p. 478, n. 413. It might also be added that the adjective, *ingens*, could be taken to imply both δεινός and ἄριστος.

27. I have omitted the words "no dream," from l. 497 of Lattimore's translation. They do not appear in the Greek, though for translation the sense virtually requires them.

28. See Leaf, *op. cit.*, I, p. 459, n. 496 for further discussion. For what role Euripides' *Rhesus* might have played in the Nisus-Euryalus episode, see p. 129, n. 1, below.

29. Schol. BT on K 496 adds: τοῦτο ἐπὶ τῶν ἀπὸ τοῦ ἔθους συμβαινόντων · ὅταν γάρ τις νυκτὸς κακῷ τινι περιπέσῃ, φαμὲν ὅτι κακὸν ὄναρ εἶδεν ὁ δεῖνα. See also J. Van Leeuwen, *Ilias*, I, p. 371, n. 496.

30. It is not impossible to suppose that some ancient commentator on *Il*. X. 496 ff. referred the reader to *Il*. II. 859, though there is no evidence for such a cross-reference here.

31. This view is set forth at some length by W. Jackson Knight in his *Roman Vergil* (2nd ed., Harmondsworth, 1966). See especially chap. 3, "Tradition and Poetry."

32. Heinze, *op. cit.*, pp. 258 ff., n. 1.

33. Macrobius *Sat.* VI. iii, 8: Ennius traxit:
    et tum sicut equus qui de praesepibus fartus
    vincla suis magnis animis abrupit et inde
    fert sese campi per caerula laetaque prata
    celso pectore, saepe iubam quassat simul altam
    spiritus ex anima calida spumas agit albas.

34. See also H. Erbse, *Beiträge zur Überlieferung der Ilias-scholien*, *Zetemata* 24 (1960), pp. 159 ff. and pp. 272 f., for further discussion of this scholium, and the attribution of the ἄχος gloss by Hesychius to Aristonicus. It is reasonable to suppose that the debate preceded Aristonicus and that the choice he presents is the one which seemed most correct to him. See also *s.v.* κριθίασις in *LSJ*, p. 995.

35. Cf. C. Beye, *The Iliad, the Odyssey, and the Epic Tradition* (Garden City, 1966), p. 27, who does not, however, cite the scholia. For a different view, see D. Lee, *The Similes of the Iliad and the Odyssey Compared* (Melbourne, 1964), p. 39. See also Leaf, *op. cit.*, I, p. 249 *ad loc.*

36. In describing the mane, Homer appears to have seized upon a primary point of comparison, for Paris was renowned for his physical appearance and for his fine head of hair. Cf. Horace, *Odes* I. xv, 13 ff., 19–20. For Turnus's pride, see *Aen.* X. 445, 514; XII, 326, and G. K. Galinsky, "The Hercules-Cacus Episode in *Aeneid* VIII," *AJP* LXXXVII (1966) p. 35. It might also be added that Turnus is described, here, as not yet having his helmet on (*tempora nudus adhuc*, 1. 489). Perhaps, too, there is a related significance in the detail of the simile which likens Turnus to a wounded lion (*Aen.* XII. 1–9), *gaudetque comantis/excutiens cervice toros. . . .*

At any rate, when Turnus arms himself for battle, he alludes to Aeneas as a Phrygian bandit (484). This simile, following directly upon the allusion, becomes rather ironic insofar as it implies that Turnus, far from another Achilles, is more like another Paris, or perhaps, though less likely, another Hector.

37. Cf. schol. BT on *Il.* VII. 214, which praise the description of the giant Ajax as he strides forth into battle, brandishing his spear which Homer says gladdened the Achaeans but struck terror into the hearts of the Trojans.

38. For Zoilus, see H. V. Apfel, "Homeric Criticism in the Fourth Century B.C.," *Tapa* 69 (1938), pp. 250 ff. For other ancient views of Homer's "fire imagery," see schol. A on E 7; T on $\varLambda$ 4; AT on M 177; T on $\varSigma$ 1, and A on $\varSigma$ 206–7. See also C. Whitman, *Homer and the Homeric Tradition* (Cambridge, Mass., 1958), p. 129 on fire as a "metonym for war." It is interesting to note that in some respects, the ancient views of imagery are quite similar to our own, cf., for example, the comments on a series of astronomical images in the BT schol. on *Il.* XIX. 374–98.

39. *Op. cit.*, p. 259, n. 1: "Helm und Schild des Diomedes strahlen hell wie der Sirius, E 4: so Helm und Schild des Aeneas, X, 272, aber hier ist geschildert, wie der Anblick auf die Feinde wirkt, der Sirius heisst *sitim morbosque ferens mortalibus aegris*, und der Unglück verheissende Komet ist hinzegefügt: also, keine blosse Veranschaulichung des Sinnlichen, sondern zugleich des Psychischen."

40. See below, pp. 41 f. and 125, n. 4 for the use of the word *phantasia*.

41. See also Servius on *Aen.* X. 270, for further comment on this description.

42. *Op. cit.*, pp. 168, n. 2, 356, and 358. Perhaps the description of *Impius Furor* imprisoned in I. 294, derives loosely from the allegorization of the imprisoned Ares in *Il.* V. 385. See schol. B as representative of θύμος or ὀργή and ἐπιθυμία. If so, and notwithstanding the remarks of Conington-Nettleship (*ad loc.*) concerning Apelles' painting, Vergil might well have utilized the allegorization rather than the Homeric myth or figure. Such allegorizations were surely set forth in the schools and well known to all serious students of Homer.

43. Schol. E on θ 267 and Servius *ad Aen.* I. 742.
44. Whitman, *op. cit.*, p. 126.
45. See P. de Lacy, "Stoic Views of Poetry," *AJP* 69 (1948), p. 262, and Eustathius on *Il.* XI. 32–40 and XVIII. 484.
46. de Lacy, *loc. cit.* "Ps.-Plutarch's" view could conceivably have stemmed from Agallis's interpretation of the shield.

Chapter III.

1. See C. H. Whitman, *Homer and the Homeric Tradition* (Cambridge, Mass., 1958), especially chap. VI, "Image, Symbol, and Formula"; B. W. Knox, "The Serpent and the Flame," *AJP* LXXI (1950), pp. 379–400; V. Pöschl, *Die Dichtkunst Virgils* (Innsbruck, 1950); S. Small, "The Arms of Turnus," *TAPA* 90 (1959), pp. 243–52; M. Putman, *The Poetry of the Aeneid* (Cambridge, Mass., 1965); see also B. Marti, "The Meaning of the Pharsalia," *AJP* LXVI (1945), pp. 352–76.
2. General studies such as G. Grube's *The Greek and Roman Critics* (Toronto, 1965) hardly touch upon the subject, which is understandable since no treatises on the topic *per se* in antiquity are extant. See, however, his remarks on "The Schools of Philosophy" (pp. 133 ff.), Philodemus (pp. 193 ff.), and Longinus (pp. 347 f.). Such comments as G. Kennedy's on the "general absence of developed criticism in antiquity," and "general failure of selfconscious analysis," while perhaps accurate in his context, are somewhat misleading and do not appear to take into account the Homeric scholia (see his *The Art of Persuasion in Greece* [Princeton, 1963], p. 8). M.-L. von Franz has carefully gathered together many fine examples of ancient views of the imaginative qualities of Homer's expression in her University of Zürich Dissertation, *Die aesthetischen Anschauungen der Iliasscholien (im Codex Ven. B und Townleianus* (1943), pp. 19–34. See especially Teil III, 2: "Das Laocoon-Problem. 'Phantasia' und 'Enargeia'. Die einzelnen Qualitäten des Stils." Many of the views expressed in the scholia, Dr. von Franz believes, stem from Stoics (p. 20) and her opinion in general finds substantiation in P. de Lacy's "Stoic Views of Poetry," *AJP* LXIX (1948), pp. 241–71.

3. See von Franz, *op. cit.*, Teil III,1: "Die Unfehlbarkeit Homers in sachlicher Hinsicht," pp. 9 ff., and p. 24 on Homer's effective use even of the sounds of words (e.g., I. 530; II. 210: III. 358; IV. 452; V. 216; VII. 208; IX. 446; XII. 798; XIV. 394, etc.).

4. Some of von Franz's references include, above all, B on *Il.* IV. 434, which she compares with Chrysippus's remarks in his *Peri Phantasias* collected in J. von Arnim, *Stoicorum Veterum Fragmenta* (Leipzig, 1903), vol. II, pp. 21 ff. and Longinus, XV. 1. Further examples are the scholia on *Il.* I. 481; II. 414; IV. 113, 126, 439; VI. 467; VII. 62; X. 139; XII. 113; XV. 695, 712; XVI. 107; XVII. 85; XX. 56; XXI. 68, 354; XXIII. 362.

5. P. de Lacy, *op. cit.*, p. 261, and especially F. Buffière, *Les Mythes d'Homère et la Pensée Grecque* (Paris, 1956), chap. III, "Allegorie et Symbolisme," pp. 45–65; pp. 52–54 contain a discussion of the serpent-sparrow omen.

6. Knauer, *op. cit.*, p. 77, n. 3.

7. We know of a Polles who wrote such a treatise, but little else seems available about him. His work is prior to Porphyry.

8. The sparrow, it should be added, was regarded as a "lewd" and "lecherous" bird.

9. Schol. AT on B 308 preserve essentially the same remarks to this point, though in highly condensed form.

10. See H. Schrader, *Porphyrii Quaestionum Homericarum ad Iliadem Reliquias* (Leipzig, 1882), Fasc. I, pp. 34 f., n. on 30 ff.

11. Some of the exegesis is quite readily apparent in Homer's description and indeed is necessary for the interpretation which Calchas gives.

12. B. Knox, *op. cit.*, p. 379. What possible influence in this matter Sophocles' *Laocoon* might have had on Vergil is impossible to say. The same holds true for Lesches' *Little Iliad*.

13. Cf., for example, BT on O, 381, and ABT on I, 4, where a view of Molo of Rhodes, Cicero's professor of rhetoric, is preserved.

14. Schol. BT on Λ 347 add, commenting on Homer's use of the middle/passive form of the verb κυλίνδεται, that he (Diomedes) knows that Hector is "possessed" of a *daimôn*:

κυλίνδεται) ἀντὶ τοῦ ἐπιπέμπεται · οἶδε γὰρ ὡς τὸ δαιμόνιον αὐτῷ συνεργεῖ. [B] κυλίνδεται ὄβριμος Ἕκτωρ) ἀντὶ
τοῦ κυλίνδει, ὡς ἄνεμος κυλίνδει κῦμα (Od. V, 296). οἶδε
γάρ, ὅτι τὸ δαιμόνιον αὐτῷ συναίρεται. This presumably
means no more than that he comes on "like one possessed,"
i.e., of an "evil spirit," such as Allecto.

15. See Aristotle *Rhetoric*, III. xi, 1411b, although his whole
discussion of metaphor is quite pertinent and would appear
to lie behind the scholiasts' comments. See also *Grube, op.
cit.*, pp. 347 f.

16. The point was made long ago and quite succinctly by W. Y.
Sellar, *The Roman Poets of the Augustan Age: Virgil*, 3rd ed.
(Oxford, 1897), p. 415, where he speaks of "imaginative
analogies."

17. This is clear if only from the reference to Comanus, a contemporary of Aristarchus; see RE, XI, p. 1126, l. 32. H.
Erbse, *Beiträge zur Überlieferung der Iliasscholien*, *Zetemata* 24 (1960), pp. 329 ff., argues, however, that Comanus
aspirated ὀλοοίτροχος.

18. Cf. schol. BT on M 46; *P* 20; *Σ* 162–4; cf. also T on N 150.

19. M. Van der Valk, *op. cit.*, I, p. 466 and n. 286, and his references to H. I. Marrou, *A History of Education in Antiquity* (N. Y., 1964), pp. 234 ff. English translation by G.
Lamb.

20. The scholia, it should be added, objected that lions do not
devour carcasses of dead animals. M. Van der Valk compares this simile to *Aen.* X. 723 and believes that Vergil "takes
into account the objections of the ancient critics, for he
speaks of a prey of a lion which is still alive." This may
very well be true, and another example of the influence of
Homeric criticism on Vergil. It is also noteworthy that
Servius (*ad Aen.* X. 724) equates *vesana fames* with *Malesuada Fames* (VI. 276), who haunts the gates of the underworld. The simile, of course, is used of Mezentius.

21. See B. Otis, *op. cit.*, pp. 372 ff. and M. Putnam, *op. cit.*,
pp. 153 ff.

22. V. Pöschl, *op. cit.*, pp. 167 ff. When Aeneas and his companions are likened to ravening wolves (II. 355), their
violentia and *furor* are emphasized in their efforts to wreak
one last frightful act of vengeance on the Greeks. This, then,

is not an exception to the symbolism implied in similes of beasts of prey.

23. Viktor Pöschl, *The Art of Vergil*, p. 99 (Ann Arbor, 1962), translated by G. Seligson.

24. It would seem that this type of observation was made particularly on similes which illustrate the character and actions of Hector and the Trojans. See Heinze, *op. cit.*, p. 259, n. 1, and his reference to W. Dittenberger, "zu Antiphons Tetralogien," *Hermes* 40 (1905), pp. 450–70, where a list of scholia that point to the anti-Trojan bias of the ancient commentators is compiled. See also H. Van der Valk, "Homer's Nationalistic Attitude," *L'Antiquité Classique* XXII (1953), pp. 5–26.

Chapter IV.

1. For recent comparisons see Pöschl, *op. cit.*, pp. 41 ff.; W. S. Anderson, "On Vergil's Use of the *Odyssey*," *Vergilius* 9 (1963), pp. 1–7; R. D. Williams, "Vergil and the *Odyssey*," *Phoenix* 17 (1963), pp. 266–74; G. Knauer, *op. cit.*, pp. 175–77.

2. Conington-Nettleship, *op. cit.*, II, p. xliv; B. Otis, *op. cit.*, p. 39.

3. G. Knauer, "Vergil's *Aeneid* and Homer," *GRBS* V (1964), pp. 61–84.

4. This short prayer, it should be added, appears to be a private utterance concerning Aeneas's own safety and destiny, neither heard nor meant to be heard by the Trojans. See Conington-Nettleship, *op. cit.*, II, p. 15, n. 94 and Servius *ad Aen.* I. 92. For a sensitive discussion of the difference of character as revealed by the prayers of Aeneas and Odysseus, see Pöschl, *op. cit.*, pp. 57–59; A. J. Gossage, "Aeneas at Sea," *Phoenix* 17 (1963), pp. 131–36; and B. Otis, *op. cit.*, pp. 230 ff.

5. See V. Bérard, *L'Odyssée*, 4th ed. (Paris, 1946), II, p. 63, who reads for line 193:

$$εἴ τις <ἐνίσποι> μῆτι<ν> \cdot ἐγὼ δ' οὐκ <οἶδά γ' ἀμείνω>.$$

This reading, which is quite arbitrary, indicates the difficulties at least one modern commentator has felt with these lines.

6. See Conington-Nettleship, *op. cit.*, II, p. 24, n. 180.

7. *Sat.* V. 11, 5 ff.

8. Servius's comment on *Aen.* I. 198: "et totus hic locus de Naeviano belli Punici libro translatus est" need be of no concern to us here, since Vergil certainly had the Homeric passage in mind as well.

9. R. S. Conway, *Vergil's Aeneid: Book I* (Cambridge, 1935), p. 52, n. 199.

10. V. Pöschl, *op. cit.*, pp. 68 ff. See also B. Otis, *op. cit.*, pp. 232 f.

11. E.g., Conington-Nettleship, *op. cit.*, II, p. 26, n. 199.

12. Cf. Servius *ad Aen.* I. 199. Vergil appears to have taken the situation from *Od.* X. 172 ff. and used the first line of the speech of the following morning (189) and the fifth (193) as the "shell" for Aeneas's address. The "body" of the speech stems from *Od.* XII. 208 ff., as Macrobius has noted. See also Knauer, *op. cit.*, p. 176, n. 2.

13. Cf. Servius *ad Aen.* I. 197; *dictis maerentia*: "bene ante epulas et hortatur socios et solatur"—a remark which has little significance except in comparison with the scholium on the *Odyssey* passage.

14. "Ἀρίσταρχος, Buttman pro Ἀρχίλοχος. Frequens horum nominum permutatio, de qua dixit Ruhnken, *Praef. ad Hesych.*, II, p. vii": so Dindorf, *Scholia Graeca in Homeri Odysseam* (Oxford, 1855), II, p. 461. On the question of the genuineness of line 189, see ·schol. H. thereto and W. Merry and J. Riddell, *Homer's Odyssey*, 2nd ed. (Oxford, 1886), I, p. 415, nn. 189 and 190.

15. See note 5, above, and M. Van der Valk, *Textual Criticism of the Odyssey* (Leiden, 1948), pp. 274 f. for a possible solution to the problem, which, however, does not effect the argument here.

16. V. Pöschl, *op. cit.*, p. 69.

17. *Od.* IX. 528 ff., Polyphemus's prophecy.

18. R. D. Williams, *op. cit.*, pp. 266 ff. in general, and in particular, B. Otis, *op. cit.*, pp. 223 ff.

19. Tiberius Claudius Donatus, in his discussion of the effectiveness of Aeneas's *consolatio* to his men, concludes:
    > namque satis reprehensibilem faceret Aeneae personam, si sine fraude hilarem diceret aut purgato doloribus corde, quem conveniebat in sua causa plus affligi quam

ceteros. dehinc ostenditur quantum potuit illa consolatio.

(*Interpretationes Vergilianae, ad Aen.* I. 205)
Such a remark would seem to be a direct allusion to *Od.* X.
189 ff., and the scholia thereon.

20. *Od.* VII. 19 ff.; Macrobius *Sat.* V. 4, 6, compares *Od.* VI.
149 ff. to *Aen.* I. 326 ff.

21. See schol. HPQ on ζ 148: αὐτίκα μειλίχιον καὶ κερδαλέον)
πανοῦργον, κέρδος αὐτῷ φέρον. See also schol. on ζ 170,
173, and 178 which discuss Odysseus's attempts to elicit
pity. These scholia, and those like them, are all lessons of
the schools of rhetoric, but all the more so for this reason
would they be well known.

22. *Od.* XIII. 228 ff. See also C. R. Trahman, "Odysseus' Lies,"
Phoenix VI (1952), pp. 31–43.

23. See W. B. Anderson, "Sum Pius Aeneas," *C. R.* 44 (1930),
pp. 3–4. Cf. also Servius *ad Aen.* 1. 327; *o quam te*: quae
dea sit dubitat, nam deam esse confidit.

24. One might profitably recall Athena's words to Odysseus
concerning his wiles (*Od.* XIII. 291 ff.) and those of Poseidon
concerning Aeneas's *pietas* (*Il.* XX. 293 ff.).

25. So the scholia comment on Odysseus's identification of himself and his ulterior motives. Compare, however, Turnus's
words of scorn concerning the wiles of the Achaeans and
Odysseus in *Aen.* IX. 151–54 and 602.

Chapter V.

1. G. E. Duckworth, "Fate and Free Will in the *Aeneid*," *CJ*
51 (1955), pp. 357–65. See also Heinze, *op. cit.*, pp. 216 ff.
and A. Cartault, *L'Art de Virgile dans l'Énéide* (Paris, 1926),
II, pp. 666–76, both of whom demonstrate how closely the
Nisus-Euryalus episode is based upon the *Dolonia*. See,
too, B. Fenik, *The Influence of Euripides on Vergil's Aeneid*
(Princeton University Dissertation, 1960), especially pp. 58–
59 for the difficulty in determining what influence Accius's
Nyktegersia might have had on this episode.

2. Cf. also B on K 11, where Porphyry preserves a similar
comment.

3. *Aen.* IX. 168: haec super e vallo prospectant Troes. . . .

4. ADT on K 194. B on 198 preserves a similar *lysis* and attributes it to Aristotle, an attribution which indicates the early origin of many of these comments.

5. Heinze, *op. cit.*, pp. 217 ff.; Prescott, *op. cit.*, p. 205.

6. Conington-Nettleship, *op. cit.*, III, p. 181, n. 230.

7. A on Θ 493.

8. A recent effort has been made to show that the terrain depicted in the Nisus-Euryalus episode fits that of Ostia. If true, this would emphasize still further Vergil's great care for every detail. It is perhaps not a coincidence that Aristarchus in his monograph on the Greek camp appears to have drawn up a plan of its site. See B. Tilly, "The Topography of *Aeneid* IX," *Archeologia Classica*, VIII (1956), pp. 164–72; schol. A on K 53; Λ 166, 807; M 258 and O 449. Cf. also H. Rowell, "Vergil and the Forum of Augustus," *AJP* 62 (1941), pp. 261–76.

9. Conington-Nettleship, *op. cit.*, III, p. 152.

10. Prescott, *op. cit.*, p. 206.

11. See Leaf's note on this line, *op. cit.*, I, p. 442.

12. The comparison with ἑταιρίσσετο seems to have no bearing on the reference to friend. It may well be simply that the scholium wished to emphasize the wisdom of Diomedes' decision to choose Odysseus. See, too, Eustathius's remarks *ad loc.*

13. It is interesting to note how the scholiasts contrast this request with Nestor's (BT on K 308): ὁ μὲν Νέστωρ τὴν πρᾶξιν ἐξεφαύλισεν, ἐπὶ φήμης ἀκοὴν πέμπων τὸν κατάσκοπον ἢ ἐπὶ σύλληψιν μονωθέντος τινὸς πολεμίου, ὁ δὲ Ἕκτωρ ἐπὶ τὴν γνῶσιν τῶν ὅλων.

14. Dolon, it should be noted, later compels Hector to swear that he will grant as his reward the horses and chariot of Achilles! See Heinze, *op. cit.*, p. 217.

15. Nestor offers a ewe with a lamb from each of the Greek nobles and a seat of honor at all feasts to whoever will undertake the deed.

16. Servius *ad Aen.* IX 192: si tibi quae posco promittunt) poscere est secundum Varronem quotiens aliquid pro merito nostro deposcimus, petere vero est cum aliquid humiliter et cum precibus postulamus. Et bene quod Euryalum nolit ducere latenter ostendit: nam ideo adiecit "mihi facti fama

sat est." The fame of the deed is all that Nisus desires for his daring: he does, however, expect to bring back *spolia* (240 ff.), with fortune permitting. See also n. 24, below.

17. One might call this an example of "double surenchère," from Hector to Nestor to Nisus. Cf. schol. T. on K 321: ὁ δὲ Διομήδης οὐδὲ μέμνηται τῆς δόσεως. See also A. Cartault, *op. cit.*, II, p. 671 for a similar view.

18. Dolon, too, is clad in skins (332 ff.). For this manner of dress see A. Shewan, *The Lay of Dolon* (London, 1911), pp. 190 ff., and for a different view, see the scholia on *K* 23.

19. See also Mühmelt, *op. cit.*, p. 132, on the *Italizusätze* in the Servian corpus, which adds, ". . . sed de illa Diomedis galea proprie intelligendum est, ut occultior sit explorator. . . ." The commentary continues to point out, citing *Il.* III. 336, that κυνέη also applies to helmets with crest and cone. Vergil, likewise, uses *galea* with both meanings.

20. The full discussion of this passage and the significance of the number of watches, which began at least as early as Aristotle (*Poetics.* 1461a, 25 ff.). need not detain us here. The criticism as quoted is sufficiently clear. See, however, Leaf, *op. cit.*, I, p. 443 and Van der Valk, *op. cit.*, pt. I, pp. 124 ff.

21. Φράσατο does not mean "see," as the scholiasts understood it. For the observations of Zoilus and Megacleides on this question, see B on K 274.

22. T on K 276: νύκτα δι' ὀρφναίην) οἰκονομικῶς · ἀσέληνος γάρ ἐστιν ἡ νύξ. . . . Through the darkness of night) Arranging (the setting) well, for the night was without a moon. . . .

23. For Diomedes' thought (divided in his mind what he would best do, . . . μερμήριζε μένων ὅ τι κύντατον ἔρδοι, lit., what most daring deed he might do), we are reminded of Odysseus's prayer to Athena as the pair leave the Greek camp (278 ff.):

"and grant that we come back in glory to the strong-benched vessels
when we have done a great thing that will sadden the Trojans."

in turn, quite similar to Nisus's desire to accomplish "some great deed" (184 ff.). Cf. also, schol. BT on K 339, quoted on p. 71.

24. Fenik, *op. cit.*, p. 81, points out that in the *Rhesus*. 665 ff., Athena must warn both heroes since they are "forgetting themselves in the slaughter" because of their eagerness. Fenik also notes, p. 60, that as Dolon sets forth on his venture, he vows that he will not return home with "unbloodied hands" (*Rhesus*. 222 f.). This is indeed reminiscent of Nisus's remark as they set out into the night (*Aen.* IX. 242–43):

> "mox hic cum spoliis ingenti caede peracta
> adfore cernetis."

See also Heinze, *op. cit.*, p. 217, n. 2.

25. See G. Duckworth, "The Significance of Nisus and Euryalus for *Aeneid* IX–XII," *AJP* 88 (1967), p. 133. While it is true that the motif of drunkenness does not appear in the *Dolonia*, Homer does speak of wine and revelry among the Trojans as they settled down for the night before the Greek camp; cf. *Il.* VIII. 545 ff. and X. 11 ff. See also X. 415 ff., and schol. BT on K 496: κακὸν γὰρ ὄναρ κεφαλῆφιν ἐπέστη τὴν νύκτ', Οἰνείδαο πάις, διὰ μῆτιν 'Αθήνης) τὸ βαθὺ γὰρ τοῦ ὕπνου δι' αὐτῆς ἐγένετο · ἔλαβε δὲ καὶ τὸ φίλοινον Θρᾳκῶν πρὸς τὸ μὴ αἰσθέσθαι.
Since a bad dream stood by his head/in the night... Oineus's son, by the device of Athene.) For the deepness of their slumber took place through her; but he [Homer?] took the Thracians' fondness for wine as the reason why they did not perceive [the Greek pair].

26. On the moral implications of the act, see Duckworth, *loc. cit.*, and Servius *ad Aen.* IX. 341: sine nomine plebem) bene expressit et bellatoris peritiam et tironis inconsideratam aviditatem; nam Nisus reges interimit, Euryalus saevit in plebem: Sallustius ex insolentia avidus male faciendi. 'sine nomine' autem dixit sine gloria. . . .

27. See pp. 70 f. for schol. BT on K 251 which points to the danger of sending out spies at such an hour.

28. On the *prooikonomia* of this line, see *Aen.* IX. 163 and SD on *Aen.* IX. 363.

29. See pp. 63 f. above and Prescott, *op. cit.*, p. 204.

30. "Fate and Free Will in the *Aeneid*," *CJ* 51 (1955), p. 363, n. 22 and A. Cartault, *op. cit.*, II, p. 696, n. 12.

31. See Conington-Nettleship, *op. cit.*, III, p. 195, n. 374.

32. See pp. 44 ff.

33. See Otis, *op. cit.*, p. 349.
34. Diomedes, of course, is frequently called a "young man" in the *Iliad* (eg., IX. 57 and X. 176); see Shewan, *op. cit.*, p. 146 and Cartault, *op. cit.*, II, p. 672 for the view that Nisus is based upon Homer's portrayal of Diomedes.
35. *Od.* I. 31 ff. See, too, Otis, *op. cit.*, pp. 349 ff.
36. "The Significance of Nisus and Euraylus for *Aeneid* IX–XII," *AJP* 88 (1967), p. 135.
37. Mention should also be made of P. Colmont, "L'épisode de Nisus et Euryale ou le poème de l'amitié," *LEC* 19 (1951), pp. 89–100, for his views on Vergil's method of imitation: "Ce parallélisme démontre ce qu'est l'imitation classique où la large part d'invention revient encore à l'originalité du poète qui imite." (p. 91).

Chapter VI.

1. On the problem of the athetesis, see Leaf, *op. cit.*, II, p. 343, n. 365. See also Pfeiffer, *op. cit.*, p. 217.
2. See Heyne, *op. cit.*, VII, p. 686, for the interpretation of the scholium as a whole.
3. Cf W. Kühn, "Rüstungsszene bei Homer und Vergil," *Gymnasium* 65 (1957), pp. 28–59. The scholiasts regarded the *Rüstungsszene* in Homer as having a relatively set form; cf. Bachmann, *op. cit.*, I, p. 20 where the A scholia to *Γ* 334–35; *Δ* 135; *Λ* 32, 41, 545; 0 480 and T 380 are cited.
4. R. Heinze, *op. cit.*, p. 229, n. 1. He omits the rest of the scholium. He remarks on the occasion: "Offenbar, weil es ihm nicht sowohl auf die Tatsache der Rüstung als auf den Charakter des Turnus ankommt: am Abend vorher, unmittelbar nach dem Entschluss, der wütendste Kampfesmut, der es gar nicht erwarten kann, die Waffen gegen den Verhassten zu schwingen; am Morgen und angesichts der Tat selbst der Abfall. . . ."; cf. Pöschl, *op. cit.*, pp. 188 f., who sees the *furor* in a somewhat different light.
5. The purpose of this *Rüstungsszene* in Homer would appear to also emphasize the divine armor which Achilles now dons for the first time.
6. The following section on the "Breaking of the Truce" ap-

peared in essentially the same form in *AJP* LXXXVIII (1967), pp. 33–44.

7. See Heinze, *op. cit.*, pp. 229–332, for a detailed and sensitive appreciation of this scene. See also the remarks in the Servian corpus *ad Aen.* XII. 176, where a few of the parallels are drawn.

8. The scholiasts also questioned Homer's use of the word διζημένη which appeared to mean that the goddess had some difficulty in "finding Pandarus." Juturna, on the other hand, has no such "difficulty."

9. Schol. B on 88 and T on 89.

10. Schol. B on 88, and cf. *Il.* III. 451, 454. For the form of this and other scholia, cf. pp. 5 f., above. Many of these problems, real or supposed, are preserved in the extracts of the scholia from Porphyry's *Homeric Problems*.

11. Cf. Heinze, *op. cit.*, pp. 230–32. Drances' harangue (XI. 336 ff.) is the one major exception.

12. Cf. also Donatus, II, *ad Aen.* XII. 225 (p. 580), for a similar comment; see, too, Heinze, *op. cit.*, p. 232, n. 1.

13 The *lysis*: δῆλον οὖν ὡς ἀποτριψόμενος τὴν κατηγορίαν τῆς ἐπιορκίας, ἵνα δοκῇ οὐ Πάνδαρος Ἀλέξανδρος δὲ εἶναι ὁ ἐκ λόχου τὸν Μενέλαον τοξεύσας.

14. Cf. *Il.* III. 86 ff., 326 ff. Before the duel begins, the Trojans and Achaeans lay aside their armor.

15. The youth, though armed (275), is less fully armed than Aeneas in his *caelestibus armis* (167). Cf. *Aen.* XII. 119 ff., where in a circumstance similar to *Il.* III. 326 ff. (noted above), all the warriors lay aside at least their shields and spears. Servius's remark on the *prooeconomia* of this detail is noteworthy (*ad Aen.* XII. 124) *instructi ferro*: bona prooeconomia et rei futurae praeparatio: ruptis enim foederibus in bella descendent: quia necesse non erat armari omnes, solis ducibus pugnantibus. As the brothers charge their enemy, Servius remarks, "Et bene a numero, a germanitate, a nobilitate, a forma, ab aetate, ab vulneris genere, ab ipsius laude, a genere mortis incitatio nata" (*ad Aen.* XII. 277).

16. The responsibility for the breaking of the truce lies, therefore, not with one man, as is the case in the *Iliad*, but rather with the entire Rutulian force, a fact which Vergil brings

out in his description of their feelings as they watch Turnus approach the altar.

17. Again, the *lysis* is of no particular consequence.

18. This point of view is made very clear by R. Lloyd in his review of M. Putnam's *The Poetry of the Aeneid* in *AJP* 88 (1967), p. 479.

19. Heinze, *op. cit.*, p. 232: "So liegt alles Gewicht auf der dramatischen Führung der Handlung und ihrer psychologischen Motivierung."

20. Büchner, *op. cit.*, p. 246: "... der Vergleich mit Homer ist von Vergil herausgefordert."

21. For further comment on this athetesis, see Van der Valk, *op. cit.*, II, p. 516, and especially n. 138; see also n. 23, below.

22. These lines, however, are allowed to stand when Talthybius repeats them to Machaon (205–7); see A on $\varDelta$ 205.

23. In this respect it is interesting to note that somone, perhaps Aristarchus, also criticized line 194 on the same grounds, as the scholium implies: οὐ περιττὸς ὁ στίχος, ἀλλ' ἐλπίδα διδοὺς τῆς σωτηρίας Μενελάῳ ὡς ἀγαθοῦ ἰατροῦ τυγχάνειν μέλλοντι (BT). The reason for retaining the line is quite valid.

24. Note the three elisions.

25. See also schol. B on X 205 for a similar comment, p. 101, above.

26. Cf. S. Bassett, *op. cit.*, pp. 34–36. See also schol. T on X 437 whose comment on a similar "flaw" in Homer's narrative technique is applicable here: ἅμα πάντα γέγονεν . . .ἀλλ' ἀδύνατον πάντα ὑφ' ἓν διηγήσασθαι.

27. See p. 101, below, for further criticism by Megacleides.

28. XII. 557 ff.: ille ut vestigans diversa per agmina Turnum
huc atque huc acies circumtulit, aspicit urbem
immunem tanti belli atque impune quietam.

29. Cf. Conington-Nettleship, *op. cit.*, III, p. 448, for the verbal parallels between the two similes.

30. W. Leaf, *op. cit.*, II, p. 56, n. 754.

31. V. Pöschl, *op. cit.*, pp. 216 f.

32. Cf. schol. AB on N 137, quoted on p. 42, above, where the word "unstable" (ἀστήρικτος) is used as part of the interpretation of ὀλοοίτροχος, and certainly implied in the under-

standing of the simile as representative of Hector's "barbaric and irrational onslaught."

33. Vergil's expansion of the simile to include the devastation wrought by the wildly tumbling rock logically arises out of the word κτυπέει (140) as well as the scholiasts' discussion of the word in question, and it is this expansion which helps make his simile all the more vivid and effective. Surely this was Vergil's understanding of the meaning of ὀλοῖτροχος rather than simply *praeceps* (684).

34. Whether or not Homer meant these two similes in *Il.* XIII to include a representation of Hector's wild fury and then of his "steady resolve" as he sets out to reorganize the scattered Trojans is not in question. The fact that the scholiasts saw a continuity between N 137 and other similes describing Hector is of importance for subsequent interpretation of the *Iliad*. See pp. 40 ff., above.

35. Aristotle also noticed this "flaw" (*Poetics* 1460a, 11 ff.), but felt that it would pass unnoticed by the reader, whereas on stage the pursuit of Hector would be ludicrous.

36. *Il.* XXII. 229 ff.

37. See Heinze, *op. cit.*, p. 483, who also cites the scholium, and *Aen.* XII. 468 ff.

38. Cf. Otis, *op. cit.*, p. 379, for further comment on this point.

39. For other examples of incidents in the *Iliad* which the ancient commentators felt revealed Homer's "partiality" towards the Greeks, see M. Van der Valk, "Homer's Nationalistic Attitude," *LEC* XXII (1953), pp. 5–26.

40. On these words, see W. Warde Fowler, *The Death of Turnus* (Oxford, 1918), p. 153. Speaking of the horror of Turnus's situation, he states: "What paralyses him is the discovery that the great deity of *fides, iustitia, pietas* is his enemy. To have Jupiter as your enemy was for a Roman inconceivable; it would mean that you are an outcast from civilization, from social life and virtue."

41. For a discussion of the athetesis, see Van der Valk, *op. cit.*, II, pp. 382 ff. It is interesting to note, too, that one scholiast saw the simile as an attempt to arouse greater pathos, presumably for Achilles (schol. A on X 201): πῶς τάχιστος ὢν ὁ Ἀχιλλεὺς οὐ καταλαμβάνει τὸν Ἕκτορα; καί φασιν οἱ μὲν ἐπίτηδες αὐτὸν ὑπὸ τοῦ ποιητοῦ καταπεπονῆσθαι

πολλῷ πόνῳ πρότερον, ἵνα ὥσπερ ἐν θεάτρῳ νῦν μείζονα
κινήσῃ πάθη . . . .

42. For a sensitive appreciation of this simile, see C. Bowra,
From Virgil to Milton (London, 1944), pp. 46 f.

43. Turnus's last act is to pick up a huge rock to hurl at Aeneas;
he adds in reply to Aeneas's taunt (894–95):

> ". . . non me tua fervida terrent
> dicta, ferox; di me terrent et Iuppiter hostis."

The irony of these words becomes still more forceful when
compared with Turnus's earlier boast after he had set fire
to the Trojan ships, which were then miraculously trans-
formed into sea nymphs (IX. 133–38):

> ". . . nil me fatalia terrent,
> si qua Phryges prae se iactant, responsa deorum:
> sat fatis Venerique datum, tetigere quod arva
> fertilis Ausoniae Troes. sunt et mea contra
> fata mihi, ferro sceleratam exscindere gentem
> coniuge praerepta. . . ."

On this point and other ironic utterances of Turnus in this last
scene of the *Aeneid*, see Duckworth, "The Significance of Nisus
and Euryalus for *Aeneid* IX–XII," *AJP* 88 (1967), pp. 146–50.

44. It is interesting to note, in the light of the traditional interpretations of the Homeric scholia concerning the simile of
the rolling rock (*Il.* XIII. 137) as symbolic of Hector's
irrational and barbaric drive, that the final scene of the
Aeneid begins with this simile used of Turnus when he
rushes to engage Aeneas (684 ff.), and that Turnus's last
act is to pick up a rock and hurl it ineffectually at his foe.

Though this is not the place to discuss the problem of
Aeneas's exit from the underworld via the Gate of Ivory
(VI. 893 ff.), through which false dreams are sent to the
world above, it is perhaps significant that Allecto first
attacks Turnus in a dream (VII. 413–58), and that this last
simile represents the nightmare in which Turnus finds himself when he realizes that Aeneas is no mere plundering
bandit as he had felt, but the instrument of fate, itself
(cf. XII. 7). Aeneas can be no "false dream," but he can
well be sent back to the world of reality as a figure misunder-
stood and opposed by those who do not realize his true
significance for the new order of things.

Chapter VII.

1. Cf. E. S. Duckett, "Hellenistic Influence on the *Aeneid*," *Smith College Classical Studies*, I (1920), pp. 1–68; M. Hügi, *Vergils Aeneis und die hellenistische Dichtung* (Bern, 1952) and more recently, B. Otis, *Virgil: A Study in Civilized Poetry* (Oxford, 1963).

2. Otis, *op. cit.*, p. 388.

3. Cf. Otis, *op. cit.*, p. 386: "He (Vergil) really does see his world in deeply emotional terms, really does transform Homeric motifs and similes into evocative symbols of his own feelings and thoughts." Cf. also K. Quinn, *Virgil's Aeneid: A Critical Description* (Ann Arbor, 1968), p. 46, where in speaking of the "significant likeness" and "significant dissimilarity" in Vergil's use of Homeric materials, he states: "Virgil seems to be aiming at something to take the place of the kind of analytic comment on character and motivation that he would have found cumbersome to express even in prose and artistically unachievable in any kind of poetic form known to him. He bends the Homeric tradition to his purpose. If Turnus reminds us at different stages of Achilles, Hector, and Paris, it is a kind of graphic substitute for psychological analysis."

4. Cf. Quinn, *loc. cit.*: "For, though so much of the *Aeneid* is taken from the *Iliad* and the *Odyssey*, nothing is any longer the same. Virgil's words constantly recall Homer, only somehow to challenge, even to reject Homer."

5. It might also be added that whereas Odysseus pretends that he suspects that Nausicaa is a divinity, in the *Aeneid*, the huntress is in reality a goddess, as indeed Aeneas devoutly believes.

Bibliography

Anderson, W. B. "Sum Pius Aeneas." *CR* 44 (1930): 1–4.

Anderson, W. S. "Vergil's Second *Iliad*." *TAPA* 88 (1957): 17–30.

————. "On Vergil's Use of the *Odyssey*." *Vergilius* 9 (1963): 1–7.

Apfel, H. V. "Homeric Criticism in the Fourth Century B.C." *TAPA* 69 (1938): 245–58.

Atkins, J. W. H. *Literary Criticism in Antiquity*, vol. I. Cambridge, 1934.

Baar, J. *Index zu den Ilias-Scholien*. Baden-Baden, 1960.

Bachmann, W. *Die aesthetischen Anschauungen Aristarchs*. 2 vols. Nürnberg, 1902.

Bassett, S. *The Poetry of the Iliad*. Berkeley, 1938.

Bekker, I. *Scholia in Homeri Iliadem*. Berlin, 1825.

Berard, V. *L'Odyssée*. 4th ed. 4 vols. Paris, 1946.

Bowra, C. M. *From Virgil to Milton*. London, 1945.

Büchner, K. *P. Vergilius Maro: der Dichter der Römer*. Stuttgart, 1956.

Buffière, F. *Les Mythes d'Homère et la Pensée Grecque*. Paris, 1956.

Cartault, A. *L'Art de Virgile dans l'Enéide*. 2 vols. Paris, 1926.

Cohn, L. "Aristarchus (22)." *RE* II. I, pp. 862–73.

Colmont, P. "L'épisode de Nisus et Euryale ou le poème de d'amitié." *LEC* 19 (1951): 89–100.

Conington, J. *P. Vergili Maronis Opera*. Revised by H. Nettleship. 3rd ed. 3 vols. London, 1883.

Conway, R. S. "Vergil as a Student of Homer." *Martin Classical Lectures* I (1930): 151–81.

――――. *Aeneid Book One.* Cambridge, 1935.

Davison, J. A. "The Study of Homer in Greco-Roman Egypt." *Mitteilungen aus der Papyrussammlung der Oesterreichischen Nationalbibliothek.* N.S. V Folge (1956): 51–58.

Dindorf, W. *Scholia Graeca in Homeri Odysseam.* 2 vols. Oxford, 1855.

――――. *Scholia Graeca in Homeri Iliadem.* 4 vols. Oxford, 1875–87.

Duckett, E. S. "Hellenistic Influence in the *Aeneid.*" *Smith College Classical Studies* I (1920): 1–68.

Duckworth, G. "Fate and Free Will in the *Aeneid.*" *CJ* 51 (1955): 357–65.

――――. "The Significance of the Nisus and Euryalus Episode for *Aeneid* IX–XII." *AJP* 88 (1967): 129–50.

Erbse, H. *Beiträge zur Ueberlieferung der Iliasscholien. Zetemata* 24 (1960).

――――. *Scholia Graeca in Homeri Iliadem,* vol. I. Berlin, 1969.

Fenik, B. "The Influence of Euripides on Vergil's Aeneid." Dissertation, Princeton University, 1960.

Fowler, W. W. *The Death of Turnus.* Oxford, 1918.

Fraenkel, E. Review of the "Harvard Servius." *JRS* 39 (1949): 145–54.

Fränkel, H. *Die Homerischen Gleichnisse.* Göttingen, 1921.

――――. "Griechische Bildung in altrömischen Epen." *Hermes* 67 (1932): 303–11.

von Franz, M. -L. "Die aesthetischen Anschauungen der Iliasscholien (im Codex B und Townleianus)." Dissertation, University of Zürich, 1943.

Grube, G. M. *The Greek and Roman Critics.* Toronto, 1965.

Guillemin, A. -M. *L'Originalité de Virgile.* Paris, 1932.

Heinze, R. *Virgils epische Technik.* 3rd ed. Leipzig, 1915.

Henry, J. *Aeneidea.* 4 vols. Dublin, 1873–89.

Heyne, C. G. *P. Vergilii Maronis Opera.* 4 vols. Leipzig, 1775.

――――. *Homeri Carmina.* 8 vols. Leipzig, 1802.

Knauer, G. *Die Aeneis und Homer.* Göttingen, 1964.

――――. "Vergil's *Aeneid* and Homer." *GRBS* 5 (1964): 61–84.

Knight, W. F. J. *Roman Vergil.* 2nd ed. Harmondsworth, 1966.

Knox, B. W. "The Serpent and the Flame." *AJP* 71 (1950): 379–400.

Kühn, W. "Rüstungsszene bei Homer und Vergil." *Gymnasium* 64 (1957): 28–59.

de Lacy, P. "Stoic Views of Poetry." *AJP* 69 (1948): 241–71.

Leaf, W. *The Iliad.* 2nd ed. 2 vols. London, 1900–1902.

Lee, D. *The Similes of the Iliad and the Odyssey Compared.* Melbourne, 1964.

Lehrs, K. *de Aristarchi studiis Homericis.* 3rd ed. Leipzig, 1882.

Maass, E. *Scholia Graeca in Homeri Iliadem.* 2 vols. Oxford, 1887.

Mackail, J. W. *The Aeneid.* Oxford, 1930.

MacKay, L. A. "Achilles as a Model for Aeneas." *TAPA* 88 (1957): 11–16.

Marrou, H. I. *A History of Education in Antiquity.* English translation by G. Lamb. New York, 1964.

Monroe, D. B. *The Odyssey.* 2 vols. Oxford, 1901.

Mühmelt, M. *Griechische Grammatik in der Vergilerklärung. Zetemata* 37 (1965).

Nettleship, H. *Ancient Lives of Vergil.* Oxford, 1877.

Otis, B. *Virgil: A Study in Civilized Poetry.* Oxford, 1963.

Perret, J. *Virgile, l'homme et l'oeuvre.* Paris, 1952.

Pfeiffer, R. *A History of Classical Scholarship from the Beginnings to the End of the Hellenistic Age.* Oxford, 1968.

Pierron, A. *l'Iliade.* 2 vols. Paris, 1869.

———. *l'Odyssée.* 2 vols. Paris, 1875.

Podlecki, A. J. "The Peripatetics as Literary Critics." *Phoenix* 23 (1969): 114–42.

Pöschl, V. *Die Dichtkunst Virgils: Bild und Symbol in der Aeneis.* Innsbruck, 1950.

Prescott, E. *The Development of Vergil's Art.* Chicago, 1927.

Putnam, M. *The Poetry of the Aeneid.* Cambridge, Mass., 1965.

Quinn, K. *Virgil's Aeneid: A Critical Description.* Ann Arbor, 1968.

Ribbeck, O. *P. Vergili Maronis Opera.* 3 vols. Leipzig, 1862.

Schley, L. "Vergils Homerisierung in der *Aeneis.*" *Wiss. Zeitschr. der Univ. Leipzig, Ges.- und Sprachwiss.*, Reihe I (1952–53): 89–117.

Schrader, H. *Porphyrii Quaestionum Homericarum ad Iliadem Pertinentium Reliquias.* Leipzig, 1880–82.

Sellar, W. Y. *The Roman Poets of the Augustan Age: Virgil.* Oxford, 1883.

Severyns, A. "Virgile et Homère." *Il Mondo Classico* I (1930): 42–55.

Shewan, A. *The Lay of Dolon.* London, 1911.

Sykes, E. E. *The Greek View of Poetry.* London, 1931.

Stanford, W. B. *The Odyssey of Homer.* 2nd ed. 2 vols. London, 1959.

Susemihl, F. *Geschichte der griechischen Litteratur in der Alexandrinerzeit.* Leipzig, 1891.

Thilo G. and Hagen, H. eds. 3 vols. *Servii Grammatici Commentarii.* Leipzig, 1883.

Tolkiehn, J. *Homer und die römische Poesie.* Leipzig, 1900.

Van der Valk, H. *Textual Criticism of the Odyssey.* Leiden, 1949.

————. "Homer's Nationalistic Attitude." *l'Antiquité Classique* 22 (1953): 5–26.

————. *Researches on the Text and Scholia of the Iliad.* 2 vols. Leiden, 1964.

Whitman, C. *Homer and the Homeric Tradition.* Cambridge, Mass., 1958.

Williams, R. D. *P. Vergili Maronis, Liber Quintus.* Oxford, 1960.

————. "Vergil and the *Odyssey.*" *Phoenix* 17 (1963): 266–74.

List of Principal Passages Cited

Aeneid

Ae. i. 197–209, p. 51; *Ae.* i. 326–79, p. 56; *Ae.* ii. 169–75, p. 18; *Ae.* ii. 203–8, pp. 39 f.; *Ae.* ii. 225–29, p. 19; *Ae.* v. 84 ff., p. 15; *Ae.* v. 327 ff., p. 15; *Ae.* v. 485 ff., p. 16; *Ae.* vi. 411–14, p. 23; *Ae.* vii. 58–273, p. 10; *Ae.* vii. 535–39, p. 20; *Ae.* viii. 626–731, pp. 34 f.; *Ae.* ix. 133–38, p. 137; *Ae.* ix. 184–87, p. 66; *Ae.* ix. 194–96, p. 67; *Ae.* ix. 226–30, p. 61; *Ae.* ix. 242–43, p. 80; *Ae.* ix. 247–54, p. 67; *Ae.* ix. 252–55, p. 80; *Ae.* ix. 267–68, p. 67; *Ae.* ix. 306–7, p. 70; *Ae.* ix. 325–28, pp. 24 f.; *Ae.* ix. 339–41, p. 78; *Ae.* ix. 354–56, p. 73; *Ae.* ix. 365 f., p. 73; *Ae.* ix. 373–74, p. 74; *Ae.* ix. 384 f., p. 80; *Ae.* x. 111–13, p. 80; *Ae.* x. 267–77, p. 32; *Ae.* xi. 486–97, p. 26; *Ae.* xi. 532–94, p. 13; *Ae.* xi. 841–47, p. 13; *Ae.* xii. 1–4, p. 89; *Ae.* xii. 1–9, p. 46; *Ae.* xii. 101–2, p. 84; *Ae.* xii. 224–26, p. 87; *Ae.* xii. 227–79, p. 88; *Ae.* xii. 311–24 ff., p. 89; *Ae.* xii. 387–91, pp. 91 f.; *Ae.* xii. 468 ff., p. 23; *Ae.* xii. 542–47, pp. 21 f.; *Ae.* xii. 570–73, p. 95; *Ae.* xii. 665–68, p. 96; *Ae.* xii. 680–91, p. 96; *Ae.* xii. 697–703, p. 96; *Ae.* xii. 742–55, p. 99; *Ae.* xii. 758–62, p. 101; *Ae.* xii. 843–95, pp. 103 f.; *Ae.* xii. 901–14, pp. 105 f.; *Ae.* xii. 931–32, p. 104.

Homeric Scholia

Iliad and *Aeneid*

Il. ii. 305, *Ae.* ii. 203 *et passim*, pp. 38 f.; *Il.* iii. 24, *Ae.* ix. 339, pp. 44, 78; *Il.* iv. 87, *Ae.* xii. 225, pp. 85 f.; *Il.* iv. 95, *Ae.* xii. 225, p. 86; *Il.* iv. 100, *Ae.* xii. 241–79, p. 88; *Il.* iv. 184, *Ae.* xii. 387, pp. 90 f.; *Il.* iv. 195, *Ae.* xii. 391, p. 92; *Il.* iv. 221, *Ae.* xii. 241–79, pp. 88 f.; *Il.* v. 4–7, *Ae.* x. 268, pp. 31 f.; *Il.* v. 613, *Ae.* vii. 535, p. 20; *Il.* v. 838, *Ae.* xii. 468; vi. 411–14, pp. 22 f.; *Il.* vi. 505–9, *Ae.* xi. 486, pp. 26 ff.; *Il.* x. 204–12, *Ae.* ix. 184–96, pp. 63 f.; *Il.* x. 242, *Ae.* ix. 184–96, p. 63; *Il.* x. 251, *Ae.* ix. 354, pp. 70 f.; *Il.* x. 258–60, *Ae.* ix. 306, pp. 69 f.; *Il.* x. 303, *Ae.* ix. 184–96, p. 66; *Il.* x. 339, *Ae.* ix. 353, pp. 71 ff.; *Il.* x. 409, *Ae.* ix. 184–96, pp. 66 ff., 75; *Il.* x. 497, *Ae.* ix. 327, pp. 24 f.; *Il.* x. 503–9, *Ae.* ix. 354–56, pp. 72 f.; *Il.* xi. 269 (347), *Ae.* xii. 684, pp. 41, 125 f.; *Il.* xiii. 137, *Ae.* xii. 684, pp. 42 f.; *Il.* xiii. 754, *Ae.* xii. 697,

p. 98; *Il.* xv. 265 (vi. 506), *Ae.* xi. 486, pp. 28 f.; *Il.* xvi. 667, *Ae.* xi.
593–874, p. 12; *Il.* xvi. 793, *Ae.* xii. 865, p. 103; *Il.* xviii. 483, *Ae.*
viii. 626, p. 34; *Il.* xix. 365–66, *Ae.* xii. 101, pp. 83 f.; *Il.* xx. 164–68,
Ae. xii. 1–9, p. 46; *Il.* xx. 389, *Ae.* xii. 542, p. 21; *Il.* xxii. 36, *Ae.* xii.
570–614, p. 94; *Il.* xxii. 193, *Ae.* xii. 749, p. 100; *Il.* xxii. 199, *Ae.* xii.
901, pp. 104 f.; *Il.* xxii. 205, *Ae.* xii. 758, p. 101; *Il.* xxii. 227, *Ae.* xii.
865, pp. 102 f.; *Il.* xxiii. 772, *Ae.* v. 327, pp. 14 f.; *Il.* xxiii. 855–57,
Ae. v. 485 ff., p. 16.

Odyssey and *Aeneid*

Od. vi. 149, *Ae.* i. 327, pp. 55 f.; *Od.* vii. 311, *Ae.* vii. 268, pp. 9 f.; *Od.*
ix. 20, *Ae.* i. 378, p. 57; *Od.* x. 185–93, *Ae.* i. 197–209, p. 53.

Servius and *Scholia*

Ser. i. 39, *Sch. Od.* i. 252; *Il.* i. 200, p. 17; *Ser.* i. 197, *Sch. Od.* x. 185,
p. 128, n. 13; *Ser.* ii. 171, *Sch. Il.* viii. 39; *Il.* iv. 515, p. 18; *Ser.* vii.
268, *Sch. Od.* vii. 311, p. 11; *Ser.* ix. 267, *Sch. Il.* x. 303, pp. 67 f.; *Ser.*
ix. 307, *Sch. Il.* x. 258, p. 70; *Ser.* ix. 341, *Sch. Il.* x. 503, 509, p. 132,
n. 26; *Ser.* ix. 365, *Sch. Il.* x. 259, pp. 73 f.; *Ser.* xii. 225, *Sch. Il.* iv.
87, 95, p. 87; *Ser.* xii. 387, *Sch. Il.* iv. 184, p. 91.